SOME FORMIDABLE GENDER BIBLICAL PARTNERSHIPS: THE GOOD, THE BAD, THE EVIL AND THE IN-BETWEEN

Lisema Walter Ralitsoele

Copyright © 2019 by Lisema Walter Ralitšoele

Epistles of Gratitude: My Thank You List to Jesus

By Lisema Walter Ralitšoele

ISBN 9781797090337

This book was published thanks to free support and training from:
EbookPublishingSchool.com

TABLE OF CONTENTS

ACKNOWLEDGEMENTS

I WOULD LIKE TO THANK GOD FOR MY FAMILY:

MY WIFE 'MATHABO EMMAH FOR CONVERTING ME FROM BEING AN ARROGANT AGNOSTIC, TO THE CHRISTIAN THAT I AM TODAY, FOR KNOWING THE TRUE MEANING OF LOVE,FOR HAVING AND ENJOYING LIFE, AND THE PEACE THAT JESUS DIED FOR US TO HAVE, IN ABUNDANCE; AND FOR CONTRIBUTING FIVE BOYS, INCLUDING TWINS, TO THE RALITŠOELE FAMILY. SHE HAS TRULY DONE HER DUTY TO GOD AND MAN:

AND OUR CHILDREN:

THABO WALTER MOSITO,

MPHO SIDNEY,

MPHOHALI SIDWELL,

TEDDY MANYEHLISA ISAIA, AND,

NTSU KHOTSO AGGREY.

IT IS THROUGH MY FAMILY THAT I BECAME A CHRISTIAN HUSBAND AND A CHRISTIAN FATHER. IT WASN'T EASY. IT TOOK YEARS OF PATIENCE AND SUFFERING ON THEIR PART; BUT I THINK WE CAN ALL SAY GOD HAS GIVEN US VICTORY.

WHY I WROTE THIS BOOK

I wrote this book because of this compulsion to share the good news of the Bible, particularly my conviction that God really had a special partnership purpose for creating a woman as the selected Biblical passages show.

The best thing about the Bible is its truthfulness; after all, being God's Word, we expect it to be truthful, and -it is- the living truth, the way and the life. The Bible reveals that Abraham lied; Elijah ran away from a woman and King David had Uriah killed so that he, David, could have Uriah's wife. Abraham, Elijah, and David were God fearing men. They were jewels in God's eye. Nonetheless, the Bible writes frankly about their human frailty.

It presents us a balanced, true view of life and not the pie- in the sky- concept that Christianity was misrepresented to be. The choice is ours-to choose life or to choose death.

Therefore, the Word teaches us to be good. It does so by presenting us with examples of people to emulate, and points the way to a good life by showing us, also by example, the pitfalls, the bad and the evil deeds of some Biblical personalities-even those who were the beloved of God- to avoid.

 The Bible also has practical guidelines for living a fulfilling and peaceful Christ-like lifestyle. So, the overriding theme is: Obedience to God's Word yields Blessings, and Blasphemy leads to Death.

The outstanding point in the following Biblical passages is that whilst God decreed the man as head of household, with undisputed dominion, however, from the beginning, woman has, as the pivotal neck, tilted the head towards epoch-making developments un-imagined by the head. In episode 1, the serpent deceives Eve concerning the forbidden fruit which she shares with Adam; the result - they are cast out of the Garden of Eden.

WHY YOU SHOULD READ THIS BOOK

This book will further add to your appreciation of how much God has used women as major change agents and thus add to your sense of self worth if you are a woman. If you are a man, you will feel honored to have the women in your life.

God used all the women in *Some Formidable Gender Biblical Partnerships* as major change agents to teach us that He is a Sovereign and loving God whom we should glorify and be blessed or choose to be disobedient and reap what we sow I hope that through this book, individuals and organizations involved in fighting the scourge of women abuse will be further empowered. The victims should find solace in the book from knowing that they come from a distinguished lineage purposely created by God and without which creation would be incomplete. If God gave such significant roles to women, we should surely give them due appreciation, love and respect.

The women differ in social status. God assigned a widow to take care of Elijah; the Virgin Mary gave birth to our Lord and Savior Jesus. Lot's daughters got their father drunk to continue the family lineage. Tamar tricked her father-in-law into believing she was a prostitute. And on the elite side are Queen Jezebel and Queen Esther.

Through this book, men will understand, and be convicted by, the fact that the abuse of women is *cannibalizing the flesh of our flesh and the bone of our bones.*

BOOK DESCRIPTION

This book is a presentation of thirteen episodes taken out of the Bible –King James Version (KJV) - that show the tremendous influence gifted by god to women. Throughout this narration, women drive men, in formal/informal relationships, to a causal outcome, good, bad, evil or in-between, that would otherwise not have been.

It is our hope that this work will instill a sense of interest in reading the Bible. The reader could have read the passages by her/himself straight out of the Bible. Here, we assist by focusing on the selected biblical passages by giving them a common gender thread that would not be deliberately highlighted in the Word of God. We believe that this makes for a more manageable and interesting Bible study.

The selected passages are mostly from action packed books of the Bible: Genesis, which is full of heroes, scoundrels, victory tragedy, and defeat. The characters include: Adam, Eve, the Serpent, Abraham, Isaac, Jacob, (the trickster) and the indomitable Joseph. Others are: 1 Kings, 2 Kings, Judges, Ruth and Esther

The arrangement of the episodes is such that each can be read independently and appreciated in its own right. This is one of the wonderful features of the Bible. You can pick any verse, and it will convey meaning and have relevance to life. All the same, an artery of obedience and humility runs through all the episodes.

God is the Alpha and the Omega. <u>Episode 1</u> is the beginning of mankind –Adam and Eve are created. The final episode is the beginning of God's salvation covenant through His Son Jesus: who is called Christ. In other words, the first episode marks Satan's deception of Eve resulting in the fall of man from grace, while the final episode signifies the beginning of the end for Satan wielding unbridled sin-power over man.

Furthermore, in episode 1, God is the Sole Creator. However, He already declares His decision to delegate some power of creation to man and woman.

In <u>episode 2</u>, the partnership of Abraham, his wife Sarah, and their bond-woman Hagar, God shows that He is still in control of the power of creation; He puts a brake on Sarah's creative system. Later on, much later on, He releases the brakes. Meanwhile, Sarah takes matters into her hand. She commands husband Abraham to use Hagar as proxy wife and she conceives.

In <u>episode 3</u>, the destruction of Sodom and Gomorrah and the consequent partnership of Lot and his two daughters, we see a bad usage of the delegated power of creation when mingled with wine, but maybe the end justifies the means.

In <u>episode 4</u>, the birth of Isaac the miracle son, God again shows us the good use of the power of creation.

In <u>episode 5</u>, the partnership of Rebekah and her son Jacob, God divulges to Rebekah, His plans for what she is bearing, while husband Isaac is ignorant.

<u>Episode 6</u>, the partnership of Jacob's sons: Reuben and his step-mother Bilhah; and, Judah and his daughter-in-law Tamar, we see the evil uses of the delegated power of creation by

Reuben and Onan; whereas in the case of Judah and Tamar, Judah had a plausible excuse and his case can therefore be considered in-between.

In episode 7 the partnership of King Ahab and his queen Jezebel and episode 8 the partnership of Elijah and the widow, we move from creation to the evil deeds and the good deeds in some gender biblical partnerships. The Ahab/Jezebel partnership is marked by the unforgivable sin of blasphemy. The partnership of Elijah and the widow, on the other hand, shows obedience that releases God's blessings.

Episode 9, Elijah's message to Ahab, shows that punishment for evil deeds is inevitable and severe.

Episode 10, Samson and Delilah, reminds us that God is still in control of His powers of creation. The episode also shows that punishment for the bad deed of his special creation, Samson, as well as for the blasphemy of the Philistines will be meted out.

 Episode 11, Naomi, Ruth and Boaz, is a wonderful story of true love.

Episode 12, Esther and Mordecai, and episode 13 Mary the highly favored and Joseph the obedient: and Zacharias and Elizabeth the righteous couple, deal with respectively, the physical and the spiritual deliverance of the children of Israel.

EPISODE 1: ADAM AND EVE

THE BEGINNING OF THE HUMAN RACE: ADAM
[26] And God said; Let us make man in our image, after our likeness: and let them have dominion over the fish of the sea, and over the fowl of the air, and over the cattle, and over all the earth, and over every creeping thing that creepeth upon the earth. [1]

[27] So God created man in his own image, in the image of God created he him; male and female created he them.

[28] And God blessed them, and God said unto them, Be fruitful, and multiply, and replenish the earth, and subdue it: and have dominion over the fish of the sea, and over the fowl of the air, and over every living thing that moveth upon the earth.

HUMANITY'S FIRST HOME: LIFE OF LUXURY IN GOD'S GARDEN

---

[1]Genesis 1:26-28 King James Version (KJV)

[8] And the LORD God planted a garden eastward in Eden; and there he put the man whom he had formed.[2]

Author's comment

Jehovah Jira: God has always provided the best for us.

[9] And out of the ground made the LORD God to grow every tree that is pleasant to the sight, and good for food; the tree of life also in the midst of the garden, and the tree of knowledge of good and evil.

[10] And a river went out of Eden to water the garden; and from thence it was parted, and became into four heads.

[11] The name of the first is Pison: that is it which compasseth the whole land of Havilah, where there is gold;

[12] And the gold of that land is good: there is bdellium and the onyx stone.

[13] And the name of the second river is Gihon: the same is it that compasseth the whole land of Ethiopia.

---

[2] Genesis 2:8-25 King James Version (KJV)

¹⁴ And the name of the third river is Hiddekel: that is it which goeth toward the east of Assyria. And the fourth river is Euphrates.

¹⁵ And the LORD God took the man, and put him into the Garden of Eden to dress it and to keep it.

¹⁶ And the LORD God commanded the man, saying, of every tree of the garden thou mayest freely eat:

¹⁷ But of the tree of the knowledge of good and evil, thou shalt not eat of it: for in the day that thou eatest thereof thou shalt surely die.

THE FIRST GENDER PARTNERSHIP, THE FIRST MARRIAGE

¹⁸ And the LORD God said, it is not good that the man should be alone; I will make him an help meet for him.

¹⁹ And out of the ground the LORD God formed every beast of the field and every fowl of the air; and brought them unto Adam to see what he would call them: and whatsoever Adam called every living creature that was the name thereof.

²⁰ And Adam gave names to all cattle, and to the fowl of the air and to every beast of the field;

but for Adam there was not found an help meet for him.

21 And the LORD God caused a deep sleep to fall upon Adam, and he slept: and he took one of his ribs, and closed up the flesh instead thereof;

22 And the rib, which the LORD God had taken from man, made He a woman, and brought her unto the man.

23 And Adam said this is now bone of my bones, and flesh of my flesh: she shall be called Woman, because she was taken out of Man.

24 Therefore shall a man leave his father and his mother, and shall cleave unto his wife: and they shall be one flesh.

Author's Comment

Women have, from the beginning, occupied a special place in God's scheme of creation. Eve went through a more refined creation process – from the rib of Adam, and not from dust. God breathed life into Eve; she had an independent spirit and she was gorgeously sculptured. In other words, God made this marriage/partnership to be heterosexual. Therefore, anything else is man – made and not God – ordained.

25And they were both naked, the man and his wife, and were not ashamed.

THE TEMPTATION AND FALL OF MAN– THROUGH DECEPTION AND DISOBEDIENCE COME THE FIRST EXILES

Now the serpent was more subtle than any beast of the field which the LORD God had made.[3]

And he said unto the woman,

Yea, hath God said, Ye shall not eat of every tree of the garden?

2 And the woman said unto the serpent, We may eat of the fruit of the trees of the garden:

3 But of the fruit of the tree which is in the midst of the garden, God hath said, Ye shall not eat of it, neither shall ye touch it, lest ye die.

4And the serpent said unto the woman, Ye shall not surely die:

____

[3] GENESIS 3:1-24 KING JAMES VERSION (KJV)

⁵For God doth know that in the day ye eat thereof, then your eyes shall be opened, and ye shall be as gods, knowing good and evil.

Author's comment

It was at this point that Satan, the Master Gossip-Monger, introduced his craft.

⁶And when the woman saw that the tree was good for food, and that it was pleasant to the eyes, and a tree to be desired to make one wise, she took of the fruit thereof, and did eat, and gave also unto her husband with her; and he did eat.

⁷And the eyes of them both were opened, and they knew that they were naked; and they sewed fig leaves together, and made themselves aprons.

⁸And they heard the voice of the Lᴏʀᴅ God walking in the garden in the cool of the day: and Adam and his wife hid themselves from the presence of the Lᴏʀᴅ God amongst the trees of the garden.

⁹And the Lᴏʀᴅ God called unto Adam, and said unto him, Where art thou?

¹⁰And he said, I heard thy voice in the garden, and I was afraid, because I was naked; and I hid myself.

¹¹And He said, who told thee that thou wast naked? Hast thou eaten of the tree, whereof I commanded thee that thou shouldest not eat?

¹²And the man said, the woman whom thou gavest to be with me, she gave me of the tree, and I did eat.

<u>*Author's comment*</u>

These must be the most profound words ever spoken by man. They sealed our fate. This is a stark naked flagrant abandonment of responsibility, by Adam, hidden behind the first BLAME GAME. Contrast this with Eve's simple truth highlighted below.

¹³And the LORD God said unto the woman, what is this that thou hast done? And the woman said, the serpent beguiled me, and I did eat.

14And the Lord God said unto the serpent, Because thou hast done this, thou art cursed above all cattle, and above every beast of the field; upon thy belly shalt thou go, and dust shall thou eat all the days of thy life:

15And I will put enmity between thee and the woman, and between thy seed and her seed; it shall bruise thy head, and thou shall bruise his heel.

16Unto the woman he said, I will greatly multiply thy sorrow and thy conception; in sorrow thou shalt bring forth children; and thy desire shall be to thy husband, and he shall rule over thee.

17And unto Adam he said, Because thou hast hearkened unto the voice of thy wife, and hast eaten of the tree, of which I commanded thee, saying, Thou shalt not eat of it: cursed is the ground for thy sake; in sorrow shalt thou eat of it all the days of thy life; 18Thorns also and thistles shall it bring forth to thee; and thou shalt eat the herb of the field;

19In the sweat of thy face shalt thou eat bread, till thou return unto the ground; for out of it wast thou taken: for dust thou art, and unto dust shalt thou return.

²⁰And Adam called his wife's name Eve; because she was the mother of all living.

²¹Unto Adam also and to his wife did the LORD God make coats of skins, and clothed them.

<u>*Author's comment*</u>

Despite it all, the Lord God did His job as Jehovah Jira! He made them, He provided for them, and He clothed them.

²²And the LORD God said, Behold, the man is become as one of us, to know good and evil: and now, lest he put forth his hand, and take also of the tree of life, and eat, and live forever:

²³Therefore the LORD God sent him forth from the Garden of Eden, to till the ground from whence he was taken.

²⁴So he drove out the man; and he placed at the east of the garden of Eden Cherubims, and a flaming sword which turned every way, to keep the way of the tree of life.

I like the way Dr. David Jeremiah puts it:

"As Adam and Eve looked back on the Garden of Eden, their physical removal from the Garden was a visual reminder of their break in their relationship with God. Despite their

dismal circumstances, God had a different ending in mind. He did not forsake His creation."[4]

EPISODIC CONCLUSION:

This episode is about the beginning of the human race: the partnership of Adam and Eve, who are deceived by the serpent into disobeying God. As a result, mankind is forever exiled from the luxurious Garden of Eden.

 We need to obey God's word. Disobedience is at our own peril. It was easy for Adam to obey when he was single. In a relationship of two people, it begins to be more complex. Now, a third imposter, Satan, only brings in confusion and disaster. So we should choose whom we associate with very carefully.

---

[4] Today's Turning Point with David Jeremiah. 1st March, 2016.

EPISODE 2: THE PARTNERSHIP OF ABRAHAM, HIS WIFE SARAH AND HER BOND-WOMAN HAGAR

ABRAHAM'S SON OF PROMISE

And the LORD appeared unto him in the plains of Mamre: and he sat in the tent door in the heat of the day; [2]and he lift up his eyes and looked, and, lo, three men stood by him: and when he saw them, he ran to meet them from the tent door, and bowed himself toward the ground,

[3]And said, My LORD, if now I have found favor in thy sight, pass not away, I pray thee, from thy servant:

[4]Let a little water, I pray you, be fetched, and wash your feet, and rest yourselves under the tree:

[5]And I will fetch a morsel of bread, and comfort ye your hearts; after that ye shall pass on: for therefore are ye come to your servant. And they said, So do, as thou hast said.

[6]And Abraham hastened into the tent unto Sarah, and said, Make ready quickly three measures of fine meal, knead it, and make cakes upon the hearth.

7 And Abraham ran unto the herd and fetcht a calf tender and good, and gave it unto a young man; and he hasted to dress it.

8 And he took butter, and milk, and the calf which he had dressed, and set it before them; and he stood by them under the tree, and they did eat.

9 And they said unto him, Where is Sarah thy wife? And he said, Behold, in the tent.

10 And he said, I will certainly return unto thee according to the time of life; and, lo, Sarah thy wife shall have a son. And Sarah heard it in the tent door, which was behind him.

11 Now Abraham and Sarah were old and well stricken in age; and it ceased to be with Sarah after the manner of women.

12 Therefore Sarah laughed within herself, saying, After I am waxed old shall I have pleasure, my lord being old also?

13 And the Lord said unto Abraham, Wherefore did Sarah laugh, saying, Shall I of a surety bear a child, which am old?

14 Is anything too hard for the Lord? At the time appointed I will return unto thee, according to the time of life, and Sarah shall have a son.

¹⁵ Then Sarah denied, saying, I laughed not; for she was afraid. And he said, Nay; but thou didst laugh.[5]

ABRAHAM INTERCEDES FOR SODOM

¹⁶ And the men rose up from thence, and looked toward Sodom: and Abraham went with them to bring them on the way.

¹⁷ And the LORD said, Shall I hide from Abraham that thing which I do;

¹⁸ Seeing that Abraham shall surely become a great and mighty nation and all the nations of the earth shall be blessed in him?

¹⁹ For I know him, that he will command his children and his household after him, and they shall keep the way of the LORD, to do justice and judgment; that the LORD may bring upon Abraham that which he hath spoken of him.

²⁰ And the LORD said, because the cry of Sodom and Gomorrah is great, and because their sin is very grievous;

---

[5] Genesis 18: 1-15 King James Version (KJV)

21 I will go down now, and see whether they have done altogether according to the cry of it, which is come unto me; and if not, I will know.

22 And the men turned their faces from thence, and went toward Sodom: but Abraham stood yet before the Lord. 23 And Abraham drew near, and said, Wilt thou also destroy the righteous with the wicked?6

24 Peradventure there be fifty righteous within the city25 That be far from thee to do after this manner, to slay the righteous with the wicked: and that the righteous should be as the wicked, that be far from thee: Shall not the Judge of all the earth do right?

26 And the Lord said, If I find in Sodom fifty righteous within the city, then I will spare all the place for their sakes.30 And he said unto him, Oh let not the Lord be angry, and I will speak: Peradventure there shall thirty be found there. And he said, I will not do it, if I find thirty there.

31 And he said, Behold now, I have taken upon me to speak unto the Lord: Peradventure there shall be twenty found there. And he said, I will not destroy it for twenty's sake.32 And he said, Oh let not the Lord be angry, and I will speak yet but this once: Peradventure ten shall be

---

6 Genesis 18:16-22 King James Version (KJV)

found there. And he said, I will not destroy it for ten's sake.

EPISODIC CONCLUSION
Sarah is old and past child bearing age. She, therefore, talks her husband Abraham into sleeping with her Egyptian bond woman Hagar and she bears him a son, Ishmael. In due course, god opens up Sarah's womb at age 90. She bears a son, Isaac, and forces Abraham to cast out Hagar and Ishmael.

 Sarah's lack of patience and complete trust in god's promise brought confusion to Abraham and pain to Hagar. We should always stay focused on God's word

EPISODE 3: THE DESTRUCTION OF SODOM AND GOMORRAH, AND THE CONSEQUENT PARTNERSHIP OF LOT AND HIS DAUGHTERS

¹⁵ And when the morning arose, then the angels hastened Lot, saying, Arise, take thy wife, and thy two daughters, which are here; lest thou be consumed in the iniquity of the city.

¹⁶ And while he lingered, the men laid hold upon his hand and upon the hand of his wife, and upon the hand of his two daughters;
the Lord being merciful unto him: and they brought him forth, and set him without the city.

¹⁷ And it came to pass, when they had brought them forth abroad, that he said, Escape for thy life; look not behind thee, neither stay thou in all the plain; escape to the mountain, lest thou be consumed.

¹⁸ And Lot said unto them, Oh, not so, my Lord:

¹⁹ Behold now, thy servant hath found grace in thy sight, and thou hast magnified thy mercy, which thou hast shewed unto me in saving my life; and I cannot escape to the mountain, lest some evil take me, and I die:

[20] Behold now, this city is near to flee unto, and it is a little one: Oh, let me escape thither, (is it not a little one?) and my soul shall live.

[21] And he said unto him, See, I have accepted thee concerning this thing also, that I will not overthrow this city, for the which thou hast spoken.

[22] Haste thee; escape thither; for I cannot do anything till thou be come thither. Therefore the name of the city was called Zoar.

[23] The sun was risen upon the earth when Lot entered into Zoar.

[24] Then the LORD rained upon Sodom and upon Gomorrah brimstone and fire from the LORD out of heaven;

[25] And he overthrew those cities, and all the plain, and all the inhabitants of the cities, and that which grew upon the ground.

[26] But his wife looked back from behind him, and she became a pillar of salt.

Author's Comment

Perhaps Lot's wife had to pass on, because she no longer could bear male children for the continuance of Lot's family tree.

27 And Abraham gat up early in the morning to the place where he stood before the LORD:

28 And he looked toward Sodom and Gomorrah, and toward all the land of the plain, and beheld, and, lo, the smoke of the country went up as the smoke of a furnace.

29 And it came to pass, when God destroyed the cities of the plain, that God remembered Abraham, and sent Lot out of the midst of the overthrow, when he overthrew the cities in the which Lot dwelt.

THE DESCENDANTS OF LOT:

<u>*Author's Comment*</u>

Our Sovereign God; He creates, cleanses His creation by eliminating the tainted, and recreates.

30 And Lot went up out of Zoar, and dwelt in the mountain and his two daughters with him; for he feared to dwell in Zoar: and he dwelt in a cave, he and his two daughters.

31 And the firstborn said unto the younger, our father is old, and there is not a man in the earth to come in unto us after the manner of all the earth:

32 Come, let us make our father drink wine, and we will lie with him, that we may preserve seed of our father.

33 And they made their father drink wine that night: and the firstborn went in, and lay with her father; and he perceived not when she lay down, nor when she arose. (Lot is oblivious to the lineage scheme hatched in the cave; God Alone is witness).

34 And it came to pass on the morrow, that the firstborn said unto the younger, Behold, I lay yester night with my father: let us make him drink wine this night also; and go thou in, and lie with him, that we may preserve seed of our father.

35 And they made their father drink wine that night also: and the younger arose, and lay with him; and he perceived not when she lay down, nor when she arose.

36 Thus were both the daughters of Lot with child by their father.

[37] And the first born bare a son, and called his name Moab: the same is the father of the Moabites unto this day.

[38] And the younger, she also bare a son, and called his name Benammi: the same is the father of the children of Ammon unto this day.[7]

EPISODIC CONCLUSION

Sodom is very evil in the eyes of the Lord and He determines to destroy it. Through the intervention of Abraham, Lot and his family are saved; Lot's wife disobeys the angel's instruction and she is turned into a pillar of salt leaving Lot with his daughters. The daughters connive to get their father drunk so he could sleep with them in order to ensure the continuance of his line.

Disobedience to God brought a prophetic and dramatic end to Sodom and to Lot's wife. She was turned into a statue of salt. The Bible is candid, and God works in His own way; after all, He is our Sovereign Father. Nothing is shocking to Him. He allowed the order "...be fruitful and multiply" to operate between Lot and his

---

[7] Genesis 19:15-38 King James Version (KJV)

daughters towards the preservation of Lot's heredity.

EPISODE 4: THE BIRTH OF ISAAC

PLEDGE FULFILLED: ISAAC IS BORN

And the LORD visited Sarah as he had said, and the LORD did unto Sarah as he had spoken.

2 For Sarah conceived, and bare Abraham a son in his old age, at the set time of which God had spoken to him.

3 And Abraham called the name of his son that was born unto him, whom Sarah bare to him, Isaac.

4 And Abraham circumcised his son Isaac being eight days old, as God had commanded him.

5 And Abraham was an hundred years old, when his son Isaac was born unto him.

6 And Sarah said, God hath made me to laugh, so that all that hear will laugh with me.

7 And she said, Who would have said unto Abraham, that Sarah should have given children suck? For I have born him a son in his old age.

Author's comment

Women occupy a special place in God's scheme of creation: He can lock and unlock their wombs.

8 And the child grew, and was weaned: and Abraham made a great feast the same day that Isaac was weaned.

HAGAR AND ISHMAEL DEPART

9 And Sarah saw the son of Hagar the Egyptian, which she had born unto Abraham, mocking.

10 Wherefore she said unto Abraham, Cast out this bondwoman and her son: for the son of this bondwoman shall not be heir with my son, even with Isaac.

Author's comment

Sarah causes Ishmael and his mother to be expelled from the Abraham Eden.

11 And the thing was very grievous in Abraham's sight because of his son.

12 And God said unto Abraham, Let it not be grievous in thy sight because of the lad, and because of thy bondwoman; in all that Sarah hath said unto thee, hearken unto her voice; for in Isaac shall thy seed be called.

13 And also of the son of the bondwoman will I make a nation, because he is thy seed.

¹⁴ And Abraham rose up early in the morning, and took bread, and a bottle of water, and gave it unto Hagar, putting it on her shoulder, and the child, and sent her away: and she departed, and wandered in the wilderness of Beersheba.

¹⁵ And the water was spent in the bottle, and she cast the child under one of the shrubs.

¹⁶ And she went, and sat her down over against him a good way off, as it were a bow shot: for she said, let me not see the death of the child. And she sat over against him, and lift up her voice, and wept.

¹⁷ And God heard the voice of the lad; and the angel of God called to Hagar out of heaven, and said unto her, What aileth thee, Hagar? Fear not; for God hath heard the voice of the lad where he is.

¹⁸ Arise, lift up the lad, and hold him in thine hand; for I will make him a great nation.

¹⁹ And God opened her eyes, and she saw a well of water; and she went, and filled the bottle with water, and gave the lad drink.

²⁰ And God was with the lad; and he grew, and dwelt in the wilderness, and became an archer.

21 And he dwelt in the wilderness of Paran: and his mother took him a wife out of the land of Egypt.[8]

EPISODIC CONCLUSION

God makes and keeps His promises. Despite Abraham's and Sarah's impatience, God delivered on His promise to provide an heir for Abraham.

Nothing is impossible with God Almighty; not even Sarah conceiving at age 90 years and giving birth to her promised son, Isaac, when she had turned 91.

---

[8] Genesis 21:1-21 King James Version (KJV)

EPISODE 5: THE PARTNERSHIP OF REBEKAH AND HER SON JACOB

A BRIDE FOR ISAAC

And Abraham was old, and well stricken in age: and the LORD had blessed Abraham in all things.

2 And Abraham said unto his eldest servant of his house, that ruled over all that he had, Put, I pray thee, thy hand under my thigh:

3 And I will make thee swear by the LORD, the God of heaven, and the God of the earth, that thou shalt not take a wife unto my son of the daughters of the Canaanites, among whom I dwell:

4 But thou shalt go unto my country, and to my kindred, and take a wife unto my son Isaac.[9]

10 And the servant took ten camels of the camels of his master, and departed; for all the goods of his master were in his hand: and he arose, and went to Mesopotamia, unto the city of Nahor.

---

[9] GENESIS 24:1-4 KING JAMES VERSION (KJV)

¹¹ And he made his camels to kneel down without the city by a well of water at the time of the evening, even the time that women go out to draw water.

¹² And he said O Lᴏʀᴅ God of my master Abraham; I pray thee, send me good speed this day, and shew kindness unto my master Abraham.

¹³ Behold, I stand here by the well of water; and the daughters of the men of the city come out to draw water:

¹⁴ And let it come to pass, that the damsel to whom I shall say, Let down thy pitcher, I pray thee, that I may drink; and she shall say, Drink, and I will give thy camels drink also: let the same be she that thou hast appointed for thy servant Isaac; and thereby shall I know that thou hast shewed kindness unto my master.

¹⁵ And it came to pass, before he had done speaking, that, behold, Rebekah came out, who was born to Bethuel, son of Milcah, the wife of Nahor, Abraham's brother, with her pitcher upon her shoulder.

¹⁶ And the damsel was very fair to look upon, a virgin, neither had any man known her: and she went down to the well, and filled her pitcher, and came up.

17 And the servant ran to meet her, and said, let me, I pray thee, drink a little water of thy pitcher.

18 And she said, Drink, my lord: and she hasted, and let down her pitcher upon her hand, and gave him drink.

19 And when she had done giving him drink, she said, I will draw water for thy camels also, until they have done drinking.

20 And she hasted, and emptied her pitcher into the trough, and ran again unto the well to draw water, and drew for all his camels.

21 And the man wondering at her held his peace, to wit whether the LORD had made his journey prosperous or not.

22 And it came to pass, as the camels had done drinking, that the man took a golden earring of half a shekel weight, and two bracelets for her hands of ten shekels weight of gold;

23 And said, whose daughter art thou? tell me, I pray thee: is there room in thy father's house for us to lodge in?

24 And she said unto him, I am the daughter of Bethuel the son of Milcah, which she bare unto Nahor.

25 She said moreover unto him, we have both straw and provender enough, and room to lodge in.

26 And the man bowed down his head, and worshipped the LORD.

27 And he said, Blessed be the LORD God of my master Abraham, who hath not left destitute my master of his mercy and his truth: I being in the way, the LORD led me to the house of my master's brethren.

28 And the damsel ran, and told them of her mother's house these things.

29 And Rebekah had a brother, and his name was Laban: and Laban ran out unto the man, unto the well.

30 And it came to pass, when he saw the earring and bracelets upon his sister's hands, and when he heard the words of Rebekah his sister, saying, Thus spake the man unto me; that he came unto the man; and, behold, he stood by the camels at the well.

31 And he said, Come in, thou blessed of the LORD; wherefore standest thou without? For I have prepared the house, and room for the camels.

³² And the man came into the house: and he ungirded his camels, and gave straw and provender for the camels, and water to wash his feet, and the men's feet that were with him.

³³ And there was set meat before him to eat: but he said, I will not eat, until I have told mine errand. And he said, Speak on.

³⁴ And he said, I am Abraham's servant.

³⁵ And the LORD hath blessed my master greatly; and he is become great: and he hath given him flocks, and herds, and silver, and gold, and menservants, and maidservants, and camels, and asses.

³⁶ And Sarah my master's wife bare a son to my master when she was old: and unto him hath he given all that he hath.

³⁷ And my master made me swear, saying, Thou shalt not take a wife to my son of the daughters of the Canaanites, in whose land I dwell:

³⁸ But thou shalt go unto my father's house, and to my kindred, and take a wife unto my son.

³⁹ And I said unto my master, Peradventure the woman will not follow me.

⁴⁰ And he said unto me, The LORD, before whom I walk, will send his angel with thee, and prosper

thy way; and thou shalt take a wife for my son of my kindred, and of my father's house:

41 Then shalt thou be clear from this my oath, when thou comest to my kindred; and if they give not thee one, thou shalt be clear from my oath.

42 And I came this day unto the well, and said, O Lord God of my master Abraham, if now thou do prosper my way which I go:

43 Behold, I stand by the well of water; and it shall come to pass, that when the virgin cometh forth to draw water, and I say to her, Give me, I pray thee, a little water of thy pitcher to drink;

44 And she says to me, Both drink thou, and I will also draw for thy camels: let the same be the woman whom the Lord hath appointed out for my master's son.

45 And before I had done speaking in mine heart, behold, Rebekah came forth with her pitcher on her shoulder; and she went down unto the well, and drew water: and I said unto her, Let me drink, I pray thee.

46 And she made haste, and let down her pitcher from her shoulder, and said, Drink, and I will give thy camels drink also: so I drank, and she made the camels drink also.

⁴⁷ And I asked her, and said, whose daughter art thou? And she said, the daughter of Bethuel, Nahor's son, whom Milcah bare unto him: and I put the earring upon her face, and the bracelets upon her hands.

⁴⁸ And I bowed down my head, and worshipped the LORD, and blessed the LORD God of my master Abraham, which had led me in the right way to take my master's brother's daughter unto his son.

⁴⁹ And now if ye will deal kindly and truly with my master, tell me: and if not, tell me; that I may turn to the right hand, or to the left.

⁵⁰ Then Laban and Bethuel answered and said the thing proceedeth from the LORD: we cannot speak unto thee bad or good.

⁵¹ Behold, Rebekah is before thee, take her, and go, and let her be thy master's son's wife, as the LORD hath spoken.

⁵² And it came to pass, that, when Abraham's servant heard their words, he worshipped the LORD, bowing himself to the earth.

⁵³ And the servant brought forth jewels of silver, and jewels of gold, and raiment, and gave them to Rebekah: he gave also to her brother and to her mother precious things.

54 And they did eat and drink, he and the men that were with him, and tarried all night; and they rose up in the morning, and he said, send me away unto my master.

55 And her brother and her mother said, let the damsel abide with us a few days, at the least ten; after that she shall go.

56 And he said unto them, Hinder me not, seeing the LORD hath prospered my way; send me away that I may go to my master.

57 And they said, We will call the damsel, and enquire at her mouth.

58 And they called Rebekah, and said unto her, Wilt thou go with this man? And she said, I will go.

59 And they sent away Rebekah their sister, and her nurse, and Abraham's servant, and his men.

60 And they blessed Rebekah, and said unto her, Thou art our sister, be thou the mother of thousands of millions, and let thy seed possess the gate of those which hate them.

61 And Rebekah arose, and her damsels and they rode upon the camels, and followed the man: and the servant took Rebekah, and went his way.

⁶² And Isaac came from the way of the well Lahairoi; for he dwelt in the south country.

⁶³ And Isaac went out to meditate in the field at the eventide: and he lifted up his eyes, and saw, and, behold, the camels were coming.

⁶⁴ And Rebekah lifted up her eyes, and when she saw Isaac, she lighted off the camel.

⁶⁵ For she had said unto the servant, what man is this that walketh in the field to meet us? And the servant had said, It is my master: therefore she took a veil, and covered herself.

⁶⁶ And the servant told Isaac all things that he had done.

⁶⁷ And Isaac brought her into his mother Sarah's tent, and took Rebekah, and she became his wife; and he loved her: and Isaac was comforted after his mother's death.[10]

⁵ And Abraham gave all that he had unto Isaac.

⁶ But unto the sons of the concubines, which Abraham had, Abraham gave gifts, and sent them away from Isaac his son, while he yet lived, eastward, unto the east country.

---

[10] Genesis 24:10-67 King James Version (KJV)

7 And these are the days of the years of Abraham's life which he lived, an hundred threescore and fifteen years.

8 Then Abraham gave up the ghost, and died in a good old age, an old man, and full of years; and was gathered to his people.

9 And his sons Isaac and Ishmael buried him in the cave of Machpelah, in the field of Ephron the son of Zohar the Hittite, which is before Mamre;

10 The field which Abraham purchased of the sons of Heth: there was Abraham buried, and Sarah his wife.

11 And it came to pass after the death of Abraham, that God blessed his son Isaac; and Isaac dwelt by the well Lahairoi.

THE FAMILIES OF ISHMAEL

12 Now these are the generations of Ishmael, Abraham's son, whom Hagar the Egyptian, Sarah's handmaid, bare unto Abraham:

13 And these are the names of the sons of Ishmael, by their names, according to their

generations: the firstborn of Ishmael, Nebajoth; and Kedar, and Adbeel, and Mibsam,

14 And Mishma, and Dumah, and Massa,

15 Hadar, and Tema, Jetur, Naphish, and Kedemah:

16 These are the sons of Ishmael, and these are their names, by their towns, and by their castles; twelve princes according to their nations.

17 And these are the years of the life of Ishmael, an hundred and thirty and seven years: and he gave up the ghost and died; and was gathered unto his people.

18 And they dwelt from Havilah unto Shur that is before Egypt, as thou goest toward Assyria: and he died in the presence of all his brethren.[11]

20 And Isaac was forty years old when he took Rebekah to wife, the daughter of Bethuel the Syrian of Padanaram, the sister to Laban the Syrian.

---

[11] GENESIS 25:5-34 KING JAMES VERSION (KJV)

²¹ And Isaac intreated the LORD for his wife, because she was barren: and the LORD was intreated of him, and Rebekah his wife conceived.

<u>*Author's comment*</u>

Again, the Lord unlocks a woman's womb, and the result is greatness.

²² And the children struggled together within her; and she said, If it be so, why am I thus? And she went to enquire of the LORD.

²³ And the LORD said unto her, Two nations are in thy womb, and two manner of people shall be separated from thy bowels; and the one people shall be stronger than the other people; and the elder shall serve the younger.

<u>*Author's comment*</u>

God shares a prophecy with Rebekah, whilst Isaac was left in the dark. Is this the beginning of women's intuition versus men's nonchalant logic?

²⁴ And when her days to be delivered were fulfilled, behold, there were twins in her womb.

²⁵ And the first came out red, all over like an hairy garment; and they called his name Esau.

26 And after that came his brother out, and his hand took hold on Esau's heel; and his name was called Jacob: and Isaac was threescore years old when she bare them.

27 And the boys grew: and Esau was a cunning hunter, a man of the field; and Jacob was a plain man, dwelling in tents.

28 And Isaac loved Esau, because he did eat of his venison: but Rebekah loved Jacob.

ESAU SELLS HIS BIRTHRIGHT

29 And Jacob sod pottage: and Esau came from the field, and he was faint:

30 And Esau said to Jacob, Feed me, I pray thee, with that same red pottage; for I am faint: therefore was his name called Edom.

31 And Jacob said; sell me this day thy birthright.

Author's comment

God's prophecy to Rebekah takes root.

32 And Esau said, Behold, I am at the point to die: and what profit shall this birthright do to me?

33 And Jacob said, Swear to me this day; and he sware unto him: and he sold his birthright unto Jacob.

[34] Then Jacob gave Esau bread and pottage of lentils; and he did eat and drink, and rose up, and went his way: thus Esau despised his birthright.[12]

ISAAC BLESSES JACOB A Mother's Treachery!

And it came to pass, that when Isaac was old, and his eyes were dim, so that he could not see, he called Esau his eldest son, and said unto him, My son: and he said unto him, Behold, here am I.

[2] And he said, Behold now, I am old; I know not the day of my death:

[3] Now therefore take, I pray thee, thy weapons, thy quiver and thy bow, and go out to the field, and take me some venison;

[4] And make me savoury meat, such as I love, and bring it to me, that I may eat; that my soul may bless thee before I die.

[5] And Rebekah heard when Isaac spake to Esau his son. And Esau went to the field to hunt for venison, and to bring it.

---

[12] Genesis 25:20-34 King James Version (KJV)

⁶ And Rebekah spake unto Jacob her son, saying,
Behold, I heard thy father speak unto Esau thy
brother, saying,

⁷ Bring me venison, and make me savoury meat,
that I may eat, and bless thee before
the LORD before my death.

⁸ Now therefore, my son, obey my voice
according to that which I command thee.

⁹ Go now to the flock, and fetch me from thence
two good kids of the goats; and I will make them
savoury meat for thy father, such as he loveth:

¹⁰ And thou shalt bring it to thy father, that he
may eat, and that he may bless thee before his
death.

¹¹ And Jacob said to Rebekah his mother,
Behold, Esau my brother is a hairy man, and I
am a smooth man:

¹² My father peradventure will feel me, and I
shall seem to him as a deceiver; and I shall bring
a curse upon me, and not a blessing.

¹³ And his mother said unto him, Upon me be
thy curse, my son: only obey my voice, and go
fetch me them.

14 And he went, and fetched, and brought them to his mother: and his mother made savoury meat, such as his father loved.

15 And Rebekah took goodly raiment of her eldest son Esau, which were with her in the house, and put them upon Jacob her younger son:

16 And she put the skins of the kids of the goats upon his hands, and upon the smooth of his neck:

17 And she gave the savoury meat and the bread, which she had prepared, into the hand of her son Jacob.

18 And he came unto his father, and said, My father: and he said, Here am I; who art thou, my son?

19 And Jacob said unto his father, I am Esau thy first born; I have done according as thou badest me: arise, I pray thee, sit and eat of my venison, that thy soul may bless me.

20 And Isaac said unto his son, How is it that thou hast found it so quickly, my son? And he said, Because the LORD thy God brought it to me.

21 And Isaac said unto Jacob, Come near, I pray thee, that I may feel thee, my son, whether thou be my very son Esau or not.

22 And Jacob went near unto Isaac his father; and he felt him, and said, the voice is Jacob's voice, but the hands are the hands of Esau.

23 And he discerned him not, because his hands were hairy, as his brother Esau's hands: so he blessed him.

24 And he said, Art thou my very son Esau? And he said, I am.

25 And he said, Bring it near to me, and I will eat of my son's venison, that my soul may bless thee. And he brought it near to him, and he did eat: and he brought him wine and he drank.

26 And his father Isaac said unto him, Come near now, and kiss me, my son.

27 And he came near, and kissed him: and he smelled the smell of his raiment, and blessed him, and said, See, the smell of my son is as the smell of a field which the LORD hath blessed:

28 Therefore God give thee of the dew of heaven, and the fatness of the earth, and plenty of corn and wine:

²⁹ Let people serve thee, and nations bow down to thee: be lord over thy brethren, and let thy mother's sons bow down to thee: cursed be every one that curseth thee, and blessed be he that blesseth thee.

ESAU'S LOST HOPE

³⁰ And it came to pass, as soon as Isaac had made an end of blessing Jacob, and Jacob was yet scarce gone out from the presence of Isaac his father, that Esau his brother came in from his hunting.

³¹ And he also had made savoury meat, and brought it unto his father, and said unto his father, Let my father arise, and eat of his son's venison, that thy soul may bless me.

³² And Isaac his father said unto him, Who art thou? And he said, I am thy son, thy firstborn Esau.

³³ And Isaac trembled very exceedingly, and said, Who? Where is he that hath taken venison, and brought it me, and I have eaten of all before thou camest, and have blessed him? Yea and he shall be blessed.

³⁴ And when Esau heard the words of his father, he cried with a great and exceeding bitter cry,

and said unto his father, Bless me, even me also, O my father.

³⁵ And he said, Thy brother came with subtlety, and hath taken away thy blessing.

³⁶ And he said, Is not he rightly named Jacob? For he hath supplanted me these two times: he took away my birthright; and, behold, now he hath taken away my blessing. And he said, Hast thou not reserved a blessing for me?

³⁷ And Isaac answered and said unto Esau, Behold, I have made him thy lord, and all his brethren have I given to him for servants; and with corn and wine have I sustained him: and what shall I do now unto thee, my son?

³⁸ And Esau said unto his father, Hast thou but one blessing, my father? Bless me, even me also, O my father. And Esau lifted up his voice, and wept.

³⁹ And Isaac his father answered and said unto him, Behold, thy dwelling shall be the fatness of the earth, and of the dew of heaven from above;

⁴⁰ And by thy sword shalt thou live, and shalt serve thy brother; and it shall come to pass when thou shalt have the dominion, that thou shalt break his yoke from off thy neck.

[41] And Esau hated Jacob because of the blessing wherewith his father blessed him: and Esau said in his heart, The days of mourning for my father are at hand; then will I slay my brother Jacob.

[42] And these words of Esau her elder son were told to Rebekah: and she sent and called Jacob her younger son, and said unto him, Behold, thy brother Esau, as touching thee, doth comfort himself, purposing to kill thee.

[43] Now therefore, my son, obey my voice; arise, flee thou to Laban my brother to Haran; [44] And tarry with him a few days, until thy brother's fury turn away;

[45] Until thy brother's anger turn away from thee, and he forget that which thou hast done to him: then I will send, and fetch thee from thence: why should I be deprived also of you both in one day?[13]

EPISODIC CONCLUSION

---

[13] GENESIS 27:1-45 KING JAMES VERSION (KJV)

Isaac marries Rebekah and they have twins, Esau being the eldest and Jacob the younger. While Isaac likes Esau and plans to bless him, Rebekah loves Jacob. She conspires and succeeds to get Isaac to bless Jacob thinking that he is blessing Esau.

Not even hunger should make us forego our responsibility.

Esau surrendered his God-given birth right to Jacob, which was an act of rebellion. We have to be patient and live by God's precepts despite the trials and tribulations. Esau lost a great opportunity to be revered by the children of Israel throughout posterity. Jacob, on the other hand, went on to have a distinguished pedigree.

EPISODE 6: THE PARTNERSHIPS OF JACOB'S SONS:

REUBEN SLEEPS WITH HIS STEP-MOTHER BILHAH; WHILE, JUDAH SLEEPS WITH HIS DAUGHTER-IN-LAW TAMAR.
Jacob was the grand-son of Abraham through his son Isaac. Jacob is the third leg of the genealogy of Abraham, Isaac and Jacob.

24 And Jacob was left alone; and there wrestled a man with him until the breaking of the day.

25 And when he saw that he prevailed not against him, he touched the hollow of his thigh; and the hollow of Jacob's thigh was out of joint, as he wrestled with him.

26 And he said, Let me go, for the day breaketh. And he said, I will not let thee go, except thou bless me.

27 And he said unto him, what is thy name? And he said, Jacob.

"Jacob, (trickster) he answered.

[28] And he said, Thy name shall be called no more Jacob, but Israel: for as a prince hast thou power with God and with men, and hast prevailed. [14]

Jacob had twelve sons:

[23] The sons of Leah; Reuben, Jacob's firstborn, and Simeon, and Levi, and Judah, and Issachar, and Zebulun:

[24] The sons of Rachel; Joseph, and Benjamin:

[25] And the sons of Bilhah, Rachel's handmaid; Dan, and Naphtali:

[26] And the sons of Zilpah, Leah's handmaid: Gad, and Asher:[15]

[19] And Rachel died, and was buried in the way to Ephrath, which is Bethlehem.

[20] And Jacob set a pillar upon her grave: that is the pillar of Rachel's grave unto this day.

---

[14] GENESIS 32:24-30 KING JAMES VERSION (KJV)

[15] GENESIS 35: 23-26 KING JAMES VERSION (KJV)

21 And Israel journeyed, and spread his tent beyond the tower of Edar.

22 And it came to pass, when Israel dwelt in that land, that Reuben went and laid with Bilhah his father's concubine: and Israel heard it.[16]

As a result, this is the final word that Israel foretold, when he was about to die, of his son Reuben:

3 Reuben, thou art my firstborn, my might, and the beginning of my strength, the Excellency of dignity, and the Excellency of power:

4 Unstable as water, thou shalt not excel; because thou wentest up to thy father's bed; then defiled thou it: he went up to my couch.[17]

Author's Comment

It is interesting that Israel seems to be concerned with Reuben's act more than with the complicity of Bilhah (Israel's concubine) at a time when women were severely punished for such misdeeds.

---

[16] GENESIS 35:19-22 KING JAMES VERSION (KJV)

[17] GENESIS 49:3-4 KING JAMES VERSION (KJV)

And it came to pass at that time that Judah went down from his brethren, and turned in to a certain Adullamite, whose name was Hirah.

2 And Judah saw there a daughter of a certain Canaanite, whose name was Shuah; and he took her, and went in unto her.

3 And she conceived, and bare a son; and he called his name Er.

4 And she conceived again, and bare a son; and she called his name Onan.

5 And she yet again conceived, and bare a son; and called his name Shelah: and he was at Chezib, when she bare him.

6 And Judah took a wife for Er his firstborn, whose name was Tamar.

7 And Er, Judah's firstborn, was wicked in the sight of the LORD; and the LORD slew him.

8 And Judah said unto Onan, Go in unto thy brother's wife, and marry her, and raise up seed to thy brother.

9 And Onan knew that the seed should not be his; and it came to pass, when he went in unto his brother's wife, that he spilled it on the ground, lest that he should give seed to his brother.

10 And the thing which he did displeased the LORD: wherefore he slew him also.

11 Then said Judah to Tamar his daughter in law, Remain a widow at thy father's house, till Shelah my son be grown: for he said, Lest peradventure he die also, as his brethren did. And Tamar went and dwelt in her father's house.

12 And in process of time the daughter of Shuah Judah's wife died; and Judah was comforted, and went up unto his sheepshearers to Timnath, he and his friend Hirah the Adullamite.

13 And it was told Tamar, saying, Behold thy father in law goeth up to Timnath to shear his sheep.

14 And she put her widow's garments off from her, and covered her with a veil, and wrapped herself, and sat in an open place, which is by the way to Timnath; for she saw that Shelah was grown, and she was not given unto him to wife.

Traits of the oldest profession: strategic dress, strategic location, and resolute language.

15 When Judah saw her, he thought her to be an harlot; because she had covered her face.

16 And he turned unto her by the way, and said, Go to, I pray thee, let me come in unto thee; (for he knew not that she was his daughter in law.) And she said, What wilt thou give me, that thou mayest come in unto me?

17 And he said, I will send thee a kid from the flock.

This has always been an expensive profession.

 And she said, Wilt thou give me a pledge, till thou send it?

18 And he said, What pledge shall I give thee? And she said, Thy signet, and thy bracelets, and thy staff that is in thine hand. And he gave it her, and came in unto her, and she conceived by him.

This suggests that Tamar was at that period of the woman's monthly cycle when ovulation was occurring and she felt the urge to have a man., and God's timing was just perfect.

19 And she arose, and went away, and laid by her veil from her, and put on the garments of her widowhood.

20 And Judah sent the kid by the hand of his friend the Adullamite, to receive his pledge from the woman's hand: but he found her not.

21 Then he asked the men of that place, saying, where is the harlot, that was openly by the way side? And they said, there was no harlot in this place.

22 And he returned to Judah, and said, I cannot find her; and also the men of the place said, that there was no harlot in this place.

23 And Judah said, Let her take it to her, lest we be shamed: behold, I sent this kid, and thou hast not found her.

24 And it came to pass about three months after, that it was told Judah, saying, Tamar thy daughter in law hath played the harlot; and also, behold, she is with child by whoredom. And Judah said, Bring her forth, and let her be burnt.

25 When she was brought forth, she sent to her father in law, saying, By the man, whose these are, am I with child: and she said, Discern, I pray thee, whose are these, the signet, and bracelets, and staff.

26 And Judah acknowledged them, and said, She hath been more righteous than I; because that I gave her not to Shelah my son. And he knew her again no more.

27 And it came to pass in the time of her travail that, behold, twins were in her womb.

28 And it came to pass, when she travailed, that the one put out his hand: and the midwife took and bound upon his hand a scarlet thread, saying, This came out first.

29 And it came to pass, as he drew back his hand that, behold, his brother came out: and she said, How hast thou broken forth? This breach be upon thee: therefore his name was called Pharez.

30 And afterward came out his brother that had the scarlet thread upon his hand: and his name was called Zarah.[18]

---

[18] GENESIS 38 KING JAMES VERSION (KJV)

As a consequence, Pharez and Zarah replaced the dead sons of Judah, Er and Onan. The question that might be pondered here is, do women have the ability to be schemers in their genes? We saw it with Sarah when she urged Abraham to sleep with her maid Hagar and later blamed him for the consequences. We saw it again with Rachel getting Jacob blessed by Isaac who was made to believe that he was blessing Esau. And now, here is Tamar tricking her father-in-law, Judah, to have intercourse with her by disguising herself as a prostitute.

EPISODIC CONCLUSION

Reuben was the eldest son of Jacob through his first wife Leah. His second wife Rachel had a maid, Bilhah, who became Jacob's concubine and bore him two sons Dan and Naphtali. Now it happened that Reuben had sex with Bilhah and Jacob heard about it.

Judah was the younger brother to Reuben also born by Leah. Judah married a Canaanite woman who bore him 3 sons: Er, Onan, and Shelah. Judah then got a wife, named Tamar for his firstborn Er. When Er died Onan Married Tamar; but he also died. Judah then ordered Tamar to return to her home until Shelah was old enough to marry her. Meantime, Judah's wife died and when he was consoled he visited his sheepshearers. En route he met what appeared to him to be a prostitute and he had sex with her. It later turned out that it was Tamar his daughter-in-law.

This is another example of the Bible's truthfulness. Nothing is strange or new to our God.

Because of Reuben's fleshly turbulence whereby he defiled his father's couch, Reuben was stripped of all excellence. We have to always uphold, love and obey God's precepts. It is amazing that through the resultant product of this relationship of Judah with his daughter-in-law should be born King David and Joseph the husband of Mary through whom Jesus, the Perfect Son of God, was born

EPISODE 7: THE PARTNERSHIP OF KING AHAB AND HIS QUEEN JEZEBEL

AHAB REIGNS IN ISRAEL

²⁹ And in the thirty and eighth year of Asa king of Judah began Ahab the son of Omri to reign over Israel: and Ahab the son of Omri reigned over Israel in Samaria twenty and two years.

³⁰ And Ahab the son of Omri did evil in the sight of the LORD above all that were before him.

³¹ And it came to pass, as if it had been a light thing for him to walk in the sins of Jeroboam the son of Nebat, that he took to wife Jezebel the daughter of Ethbaal king of the Zidonians, and went and served Baal, and worshipped him.

³² And he reared up an altar for Baal in the house of Baal, which he had built in Samaria.

³³ And Ahab made a grove; and Ahab did more to provoke the LORD God of Israel to anger than all the kings of Israel that were before him.[19]

---

[19] 1 KINGS 16:29-34 KING JAMES VERSION (KJV)

And Elijah the Tishbite, who was of the inhabitants of Gilead, said unto Ahab, As the LORD God of Israel liveth, before whom I stand; there shall not be dew nor rain these years, but according to my word.

2 And the word of the LORD came unto him, saying,

3 Get thee hence, and turn thee eastward, and hide thyself by the brook Cherith that is before Jordan.

4 And it shall be that thou shalt drink of the brook; and I have commanded the ravens to feed thee there.

5 So he went and did according unto the word of the LORD: for he went and dwelt by the brook Cherith that is before Jordan.

6 And the ravens brought him bread and flesh in the morning, and bread and flesh in the evening; and he drank of the brook.

[7] And it came to pass after a while, that the brook dried up, because there had been no rain in the land.[20]

EPISODIC CONCLUSION
 Ahab did more to provoke the LORD God of Israel to anger than all the kings of Israel who were before him. He served Baal and worshiped him. He set up an altar for Baal in the temple of Baal. And he made a wooden image.

The prophet Elijah warned him of a 3-year drought.

As a revelation is made to us by a man of God, we should be ready to repent or face the dire consequences.

---

[20] 1 KINGS 17:1-23 KING JAMES VERSION (KJV)

EPISODE 8: THE PARTNERSHIP OF ELIJAH AND THE WIDOW:

TESTIMONY TO GOD'S GREATNESS

8 And the word of the LORD came unto him, saying,

9 Arise, get thee to Zarephath, which belongeth to Zidon, and dwell there: behold, I have commanded a widow woman there to sustain thee.

10 So he arose and went to Zarephath. And when he came to the gate of the city, behold, the widow woman was there gathering of sticks: and he called to her, and said, Fetch me, I pray thee, a little water in a vessel that I may drink.

11 And as she was going to fetch it, he called to her, and said, bring me, I pray thee, a morsel of bread in thine hand.

12 And she said, As the LORD thy God liveth, I have not a cake, but an handful of meal in a barrel, and a little oil in a cruse: and, behold, I am gathering two sticks, that I may go in and dress it for me and my son, that we may eat it, and die.

13 And Elijah said unto her, Fear not; go and do as thou hast said: but make me thereof a little cake first, and bring it unto me and after make for thee and for thy son.

14 For thus saith the Lord God of Israel, The barrel of meal shall not waste, neither shall the cruse of oil fail, until the day that the Lord sendeth rain upon the earth.

15 And she went and did according to the saying of Elijah: and she, and he, and her house, did eat many days.

16 And the barrel of meal wasted not, neither did the cruse of oil fail, according to the word of the Lord, which he spake by Elijah.21

------

21 *1 Kings 17:8-15*

Elijah Revives the Widow's Son

¹⁷ And it came to pass after these things that the son of the woman, the mistress of the house, fell sick; and his sickness was so sore, that there was no breath left in him.

¹⁸ And she said unto Elijah, What have I to do with thee, O thou man of God? art thou come unto me to call my sin to remembrance, and to slay my son?

¹⁹ And he said unto her, Give me thy son. And he took him out of her bosom, and carried him up into a loft, where he abode, and laid him upon his own bed.

²⁰ And he cried unto the Lord, and said, O Lord my God, hast thou also brought evil upon the widow with whom I sojourn, by slaying her son?

²¹ And he stretched himself upon the child three times, and cried unto the Lord, and said, O Lord my God, I pray thee, let this child's soul come into him again.

[22] And the LORD heard the voice of Elijah; and the soul of the child came into him again, and he revived.

[23] And Elijah took the child, and brought him down out of the chamber into the house, and delivered him unto his mother: and Elijah said, See, thy son liveth.[22]

EPISODIC CONCLUSION

God instructs the prophet Elijah to go and stay at Zarephath where he would be taken care of by a widow. Whilst with the widow, she obeys him. She serves him, first, a meal out of her scanty resources. The resources are miraculously replenished. The widow's son dies; however, by God's grace, Elijah prays God and the boy's life is restored.

Obedience to God's word through faith brought the widow abundance and a miracle restoration of her son's life.

---

[22] *1 KINGS 17:17-23*

EPISODE 9: ELIJAH'S MESSAGE TO AHAB

And it came to pass after many days, that the word of the LORD came to Elijah in the third year, saying, Go, shew thyself unto Ahab; and I will send rain upon the earth.

2 And Elijah went to shew himself unto Ahab. And there was a sore famine in Samaria.

3 And Ahab called Obadiah, which was the governor of his house. (Now Obadiah feared the LORD greatly:

4 For it was so, when Jezebel cut off the prophets of the LORD, that Obadiah took an hundred prophets, and hid them by fifty in a cave, and fed them with bread and water.)

5 And Ahab said unto Obadiah; Go into the land, unto all fountains of water, and unto all brooks: peradventure we may find grass to save the horses and mules alive, that we lose not all the beasts.

6 So they divided the land between them to pass throughout it: Ahab went one way by himself, and Obadiah went another way by himself.

[7] And as Obadiah was in the way, behold, Elijah met him: and he knew him, and fell on his face, and said, Art thou that my lord Elijah?

[8] And he answered him, I am: go, tell thy lord, Behold, Elijah is here. [23]

ELIJAH CHALLENGES KING AHAB AND THE BAAL PROPHETS

[17] And it came to pass, when Ahab saw Elijah, that Ahab said unto him, Art thou he that troubleth Israel?

[18] And he answered, I have not troubled Israel; but thou, and thy father's house, in that ye have forsaken the commandments of the LORD, and thou hast followed Baalim.

[19] Now therefore send, and gather to me all Israel unto Mount Carmel, and the prophets of Baal four hundred and fifty, and the prophets of the groves four hundred, which eat at Jezebel's table.

ELIJAH'S MOUNT CARMEL VICTORY

[20] So Ahab sent unto all the children of Israel, and gathered the prophets together unto Mount Carmel.

---

[23] 1 Kings 18:1-8 King James Version (KJV)

²¹ And Elijah came unto all the people, and said, How long halt ye between two opinions? If the L ORD be God, follow Him: but if Baal, then follow him. And the people answered him not a word.

²² Then said Elijah unto the people, I, even I only, remain a prophet of the L ORD; but Baal's prophets are four hundred and fifty men.

²³ Let them therefore give us two bullocks; and let them choose one bullock for themselves, and cut it in pieces, and lay it on wood, and put no fire under: and I will dress the other bullock, and lay it on wood, and put no fire under:

²⁴ And call ye on the name of your gods, and I will call on the name of the L ORD: and the God that answereth by fire let him be God. And all the people answered and said, It is well spoken.

²⁵ And Elijah said unto the prophets of Baal, Choose you one bullock for yourselves, and dress it first; for ye are many; and call on the name of your gods, but put no fire under.

²⁶ And they took the bullock which was given them, and they dressed it, and called on the name of Baal from morning even until noon, saying, O Baal, hear us. But there was no voice, nor any that answered. And they leaped upon the altar which was made.

27 And it came to pass at noon, that Elijah mocked them, and said, Cry aloud: for he is a god; either he is talking, or he is pursuing, or he is in a journey, or peradventure he sleepeth, and must be awaked.

28 And they cried aloud, and cut themselves after their manner with knives and lancets, till the blood gushed out upon them.

29 And it came to pass, when midday was past, and they prophesied until the time of the offering of the evening sacrifice, that there was neither voice, nor any to answer, nor any that regarded.

30 And Elijah said unto all the people, Come near unto me. And all the people came near unto him. And he repaired the altar of the LORD that was broken down.

31 And Elijah took twelve stones, according to the number of the tribes of the sons of Jacob, unto whom the word of the LORD came, saying, Israel shall be thy name:

32 And with the stones he built an altar in the name of the LORD: and he made a trench about the altar, as great as would contain two measures of seed.

33 And he put the wood in order, and cut the bullock in pieces, and laid him on the wood, and said, Fill four barrels with water, and pour it on the burnt sacrifice, and on the wood.

34 And he said, Do it the second time. And they did it the second time. And he said, Do it the third time. And they did it the third time.

35 And the water ran round about the altar; and he filled the trench also with water.

36 And it came to pass at the time of the offering of the evening sacrifice, that Elijah the prophet came near, and said, LORD God of Abraham, Isaac, and of Israel, let it be known this day that thou art God in Israel, and that I am thy servant, and that I have done all these things at thy word. 37 Hear me, O LORD, hear me, that this people may know that thou art the LORD God, and that thou hast turned their heart back again.

38 Then the fire of the LORD fell, and consumed the burnt sacrifice, and the wood, and the stones, and the dust, and licked up the water that was in the trench.

39 And when all the people saw it, they fell on their faces: and they said, The LORD, he is the God; the LORD, he is the God.

40 And Elijah said unto them, Take the prophets of Baal; let not one of them escape. And they took them: and Elijah brought them down to the brook Kishon, and slew them there.

THE DROUGHT ENDS

41 And Elijah said unto Ahab, Get thee up, eat and drink; for there is a sound of abundance of rain.

42 So Ahab went up to eat and to drink. And Elijah went up to the top of Carmel; and he cast himself down upon the earth, and put his face between his knees,

43 And said to his servant, Go up now, look toward the sea. And he went up, and looked, and said, There is nothing. And he said, Go again seven times.

44 And it came to pass at the seventh time, that he said, Behold, there arises a little cloud out of the sea, like a man's hand. And he said, Go up, say unto Ahab, Prepare thy chariot, and get thee down that the rain stop thee not.

45 And it came to pass in the mean while, that the heaven was black with clouds and wind, and there was a great rain. And Ahab rode, and went to Jezreel.

46 And the hand of the LORD was on Elijah; and he girded up his loins, and ran before Ahab to the entrance of Jezreel.[24]

ELIJAH ESCAPES FROM JEZEBEL

And Ahab told Jezebel all that Elijah had done, and withal how he had slain all the prophets with the sword.

2 Then Jezebel sent a messenger unto Elijah, saying, So let the gods do to me, and more also, if I make not thy life as the life of one of them by tomorrow about this time.

3 And when he saw that, he arose, and went for his life, and came to Beersheba, which belongeth to Judah, and left his servant there.[25]

AHAB COVETS NABOTH'S VINEYARD, AND JEZEBEL CONSPIRES TO MURDER HIM

And it came to pass after these things, that Naboth the Jezreelite had a vineyard, which was in Jezreel, hard by the palace of Ahab king of Samaria.

2 And Ahab spake unto Naboth, saying, Give me thy vineyard, that I may have it for a garden of herbs, because it is near unto my house: and I

---

[24] 1 Kings 18:17-46 King James Version (KJV)
[25] 1 Kings 19:1-3 King James Version (KJV)

will give thee for it a better vineyard than it; or, if it seem good to thee, I will give thee the worth of it in money.

3 And Naboth said to Ahab, The Lord forbid it me, that I should give the inheritance of my fathers unto thee.

4 And Ahab came into his house heavy and displeased because of the word which Naboth the Jezreelite had spoken to him: for he had said, I will not give thee the inheritance of my fathers. And he laid him down upon his bed, and turned away his face, and would eat no bread.

5 But Jezebel his wife came to him, and said unto him, why is thy spirit so sad, that thou eatest no bread?

6 And he said unto her, because I spake unto Naboth the Jezreelite, and said unto him, give me thy vineyard for money; or else, if it please thee, I will give thee another vineyard for it: and he answered, I will not give thee my vineyard.

7 And Jezebel his wife said unto him, Dost thou now govern the kingdom of Israel? Arise, and eat bread, and let thine heart be merry: I will give thee the vineyard of Naboth the Jezreelite.

8 So she wrote letters in Ahab's name, and sealed them with his seal, and sent the letters

unto the elders and to the nobles that were in his city, dwelling with Naboth.

9 And she wrote in the letters, saying, Proclaim a fast, and set Naboth on high among the people:

10 And set two men, sons of Belial, before him, to bear witness against him, saying, Thou didst blaspheme God and the king. And then carry him out, and stone him, that he may die.

11 And the men of his city, even the elders and the nobles who were the inhabitants in his city, did as Jezebel had sent unto them, and as it was written in the letters which she had sent unto them.

12 They proclaimed a fast, and set Naboth on high among the people.

13 And there came in two men, children of Belial, and sat before him: and the men of Belial witnessed against him, even against Naboth, in the presence of the people, saying, Naboth did blaspheme God and the king. Then they carried him forth out of the city, and stoned him with stones, that he died.

14 Then they sent to Jezebel, saying, Naboth is stoned, and is dead.

15 And it came to pass, when Jezebel heard that Naboth was stoned, and was dead, that Jezebel said to Ahab, Arise, take possession of the vineyard of Naboth the Jezreelite, which he refused to give thee for money: for Naboth is not alive, but dead.

16 And it came to pass, when Ahab heard that Naboth was dead, that Ahab rose up to go down to the vineyard of Naboth the Jezreelite, to take possession of it.

THE LORD CONDEMNS AHAB

17 And the word of the LORD came to Elijah the Tishbite, saying,

18 Arise, go down to meet Ahab king of Israel, which is in Samaria: behold, he is in the vineyard of Naboth, whither he is gone down to possess it.

19 And thou shalt speak unto him, saying, Thus saith the LORD, Hast thou killed, and also taken possession? And thou shalt speak unto him, saying, Thus saith the LORD, In the place where dogs licked the blood of Naboth shall dogs lick thy blood, even thine.

20 And Ahab said to Elijah, Hast thou found me, O mine enemy? And he answered, I have found

thee: because thou hast sold thyself to work evil in the sight of the Lord.

21 Behold, I will bring evil upon thee, and will take away thy posterity, and will cut off from Ahab him that pisseth against the wall, and him that is shut up and left in Israel,

22 And will make thine house like the house of Jeroboam the son of Nebat, and like the house of Baasha the son of Ahijah, for the provocation wherewith thou hast provoked me to anger, and made Israel to sin.

23 And of Jezebel also spake the Lord, saying, The dogs shall eat Jezebel by the wall of Jezreel.26

AHAB DIES IN BATTLE

29 So the king of Israel and Jehoshaphat the king of Judah went up to Ramothgilead.

30 And the king of Israel said unto Jehoshaphat, I will disguise myself, and enter into the battle; but put thou on thy robes. And the king of Israel disguised himself, and went into the battle.

31 But the king of Syria commanded his thirty and two captains that had rule over his chariots,

---

26 1 Kings 21:1-23 King James Version (KJV)

saying, Fight neither with small nor great, save only with the king of Israel.

32 And it came to pass, when the captains of the chariots saw Jehoshaphat, that they said, Surely it is the king of Israel. And they turned aside to fight against him: and Jehoshaphat cried out.

33 And it came to pass, when the captains of the chariots perceived that it was not the king of Israel that they turned back from pursuing him.

34 And a certain man drew a bow at a venture, and smote the king of Israel between the joints of the harness: wherefore he said unto the driver of his chariot, Turn thine hand, and carry me out of the host; for I am wounded.

35 And the battle increased that day: and the king was stayed up in his chariot against the Syrians, and died at even: and the blood ran out of the wound into the midst of the chariot.

36 And there went a proclamation throughout the host about the going down of the sun, saying, Every man to his city, and every man to his own country.

37 So the king died, and was brought to Samaria; and they buried the king in Samaria.

[38] And one washed the chariot in the pool of Samaria; and the dogs licked up his blood; and they washed his armour; according unto the word of the LORD which he spake.[27]

JEZEBEL'S VIOLENT DEATH

2 KINGS 9: 30-37 KING JAMES VERSION (KJV)

[30] And when Jehu was come to Jezreel, Jezebel heard of it; and she painted her face, and tired her head, and looked out at a window.

[31] And as Jehu entered in at the gate, she said, Had Zimri peace, who slew his master?

[32] And he lifted up his face to the window, and said, Who is on my side? who? And there looked out to him two or three eunuchs.

[33] And he said, Throw her down. So they threw her down: and some of her blood was sprinkled on the wall, and on the horses: and he trode her under foot.

[34] And when he was come in, he did eat and drink, and said, Go, see now this cursed woman, and bury her: for she is a king's daughter.

---

[27] 1 Kings 22: 29-38 King James Version (KJV)

³⁵ And they went to bury her: but they found no more of her than the skull, and the feet, and the palms of her hands.

³⁶ Wherefore they came again, and told him. And he said, This is the word of the Lord, which he spake by his servant Elijah the Tishbite, saying, In the portion of Jezreel shall dogs eat the flesh of Jezebel:

³⁷ And the carcase of Jezebel shall be as dung upon the face of the field in the portion of Jezreel; so that they shall not say, this is Jezebel.

Author's comment

When women abuse God's gifting, committing blasphemous acts, the punishment is extremely severe indeed.

Episodic Conclusion

The Prophet Elijah instructs King Ahab: You have forsaken the commandments of the Lord and have followed the Baals. Now therefore, send and gather all Israel to me on Mount Carmel, and the four hundred and fifty prophets of Baal.

Naboth refused to surrender his blessing, his land, to the evil King Ahab despite monetary enticement. For this refusal Naboth was killed.

Punishment for this injustice and for blasphemy was extremely dramatic. Ahab was slain by a stray arrow and his blood was licked by dogs, and the Bible says "...while the harlots bathed." Queen Jezebel was thrown down, by eunuchs, from the top of a building through a window, trampled by a horse, on purpose, and her body consumed by dogs.

God gives us the strength to carry out His will. Elijah single-handedly executed 450 Baal prophets.

EPISODE 10: SAMSON AND DELILAH

THE BIRTH OF SAMSON

And the children of Israel did evil again in the sight of the LORD; and the LORD delivered them into the hand of the Philistines forty years.

2 And there was a certain man of Zorah, of the family of the Danites, whose name was Manoah; and his wife was barren, and bare not.

3 And the angel of the LORD appeared unto the woman, and said unto her, Behold now, thou art barren, and bearest not: but thou shalt conceive, and bear a son.

4 Now therefore beware, I pray thee, and drink not wine nor strong drink, and eat not any unclean thing:

5 For, lo, thou shalt conceive, and bear a son; and no razor shall come on his head: for the child shall be a Nazarite unto God from the womb: and he shall begin to deliver Israel out of the hand of the Philistines.[28]

---

[28] Judges 13:1-5 King James Version (KJV)

²⁴ And the woman bare a son, and called his name Samson: and the child grew, and the LORD blessed him.

²⁵ And the Spirit of the LORD began to move him at times in the camp of Dan between Zorah and Eshtaol.

SAMSON'S PHILISTINE WIFE

And Samson went down to Timnath, and saw a woman in Timnath of the daughters of the Philistines.

² And he came up, and told his father and his mother, and said I have seen a woman in Timnath of the daughters of the Philistines: now therefore get her for me to wife.

³ Then his father and his mother said unto him, Is there never a woman among the daughters of thy brethren, or among all my people, that thou goest to take a wife of the uncircumcised Philistines? And Samson said unto his father; Get her for me; for she pleaseth me well.

⁴ But his father and his mother knew not that it was of the LORD, that he sought an occasion against the Philistines: for at that time the Philistines had dominion over Israel.

⁵ Then went Samson down, and his father and his mother, to Timnath, and came to the vineyards of Timnath: and, behold, a young lion roared against him.

⁶ And the Spirit of the LORD came mightily upon him, and he rent him as he would have rent a kid, and he had nothing in his hand: but he told not his father or his mother what he had done.

⁷ And he went down, and talked with the woman; and she pleased Samson well.

⁸ And after a time he returned to take her, and he turned aside to see the carcase of the lion: and, behold, there was a swarm of bees and honey in the carcase of the lion.

⁹ And he took thereof in his hands, and went on eating, and came to his father and mother, and he gave them, and they did eat: but he told not them that he had taken the honey out of the carcase of the lion.

¹⁰ So his father went down unto the woman: and Samson made there a feast; for so used the young men to do.

¹¹ And it came to pass, when they saw him that they brought thirty companions to be with him.

12 And Samson said unto them, I will now put forth a riddle unto you: if ye can certainly declare it me within the seven days of the feast, and find it out, then I will give you thirty sheets and thirty change of garments:

13 But if ye cannot declare it me, then shall ye give me thirty sheets and thirty change of garments. And they said unto him; Put forth thy riddle, that we may hear it.

14 And he said unto them, Out of the eater came forth meat, and out of the strong came forth sweetness. And they could not in three days expound the riddle.

15 And it came to pass on the seventh day that they said unto Samson's wife entice thy husband, that he may declare unto us the riddle, lest we burn thee and thy father's house with fire: have ye called us to take that we have? Is it not so?

16 And Samson's wife wept before him, and said, Thou dost but hate me, and lovest me not: thou hast put forth a riddle unto the children of my people, and hast not told it me. And he said unto her, Behold, I have not told it my father nor my mother, and shall I tell it thee?

17 And she wept before him the seven days, while their feast lasted: and it came to pass on

the seventh day, that he told her, because she
lay sore upon him: and she told the riddle to the
children of her people.

18 And the men of the city said unto him on the
seventh day before the sun went down, what is
sweeter than honey? And what is stronger than
a lion? And he said unto them, if ye had not
plowed with my heifer, ye had not found out my
riddle.

19 And the Spirit of the LORD came upon him, and
he went down to Ashkelon, and slew thirty men
of them, and took their spoil, and gave change of
garments unto them which expounded the
riddle. And his anger was kindled, and he went
up to his father's house.

20 But Samson's wife was given to his
companion, whom he had used as his friend.29

14 And when he came unto Lehi, the Philistines
shouted against him: and the Spirit of
the LORD came mightily upon him, and the cords
that were upon his arms became as flax that
was burnt with fire, and his bands loosed from
off his hands.

15 And he found a new jawbone of an ass, and
put forth his hand, and took it, and slew a
thousand men therewith.

---

29 Judges 14:1-20 King James Version (KJV)

16 And Samson said, With the jawbone of an ass, heaps upon heaps, with the jaw of an ass have I slain a thousand men.

17 And it came to pass, when he had made an end of speaking, that he cast away the jawbone out of his hand, and called that place Ramathlehi.

18 And he was sore athirst, and called on the LORD, and said, Thou hast given this great deliverance into the hand of thy servant: and now shall I die for thirst, and fall into the hand of the uncircumcised?

19 But God clave an hollow place that was in the jaw, and there came water thereout; and when he had drunk, his spirit came again, and he revived: wherefore he called the name thereof Enhakkore, which is in Lehi unto this day.

20 And he judged Israel in the days of the Philistines twenty years.30

SAMSON THE AVENGER OF GOD'S PEOPLE *AND DELILAH:* THE BETRAYER

Then went Samson to Gaza, and saw there an harlot, and went in unto her.

---

30 Judges 15:14-20 King James Version (KJV)

² And it was told the Gazites, saying, Samson is come hither. And they compassed him in, and laid wait for him all night in the gate of the city, and were quiet all the night, saying, In the morning, when it is day, we shall kill him.

³ And Samson lay till midnight, and arose at midnight, and took the doors of the gate of the city, and the two posts, and went away with them, bar and all, and put them upon his shoulders, and carried them up to the top of an hill that is before Hebron.

⁴ And it came to pass afterward, that he loved a woman in the valley of Sorek, whose name was Delilah.

⁵ And the lords of the Philistines came up unto her, and said unto her, Entice him, and see wherein his great strength lieth, and by what means we may prevail against him, that we may bind him to afflict him; and we will give thee every one of us eleven hundred pieces of silver.

Author's comment

Unbeknown to Samson, Delilah betrayed him for a hefty fee; but the Son of Man knew beforehand that His very own follower Judas, was going to betray Him: and, yet, He continued to do His Father's Will.

6 And Delilah said to Samson, Tell me, I pray thee, wherein thy great strength lieth, and wherewith thou mightest be bound to afflict thee.

7 And Samson said unto her, If they bind me with seven green withs that were never dried, then shall I be weak, and be as another man.

8 Then the lords of the Philistines brought up to her seven green withs which had not been dried and she bound him with them.

9 Now there were men lying in wait, abiding with her in the chamber. And she said unto him, The Philistines be upon thee, Samson. And he brake the withs, as a thread of tow is broken when it toucheth the fire. So his strength was not known.

10 And Delilah said unto Samson, Behold, thou hast mocked me, and told me lies: now tell me, I pray thee, wherewith thou mightest be bound.

11 And he said unto her, If they bind me fast with new ropes that never were occupied, then shall I be weak, and be as another man.

12 Delilah therefore took new ropes, and bound him therewith, and said unto him, The Philistines be upon thee, Samson. And there

were liers in wait abiding in the chamber. And he brake them from off his arms like a thread.

13 And Delilah said unto Samson, Hitherto thou hast mocked me, and told me lies: tell me wherewith thou mightest be bound. And he said unto her, If thou weavest the seven locks of my head with the web.

14 And she fastened it with the pin, and said unto him, The Philistines be upon thee, Samson. And he awaked out of his sleep, and went away with the pin of the beam, and with the web.

15 And she said unto him, how canst thou say, I love thee, when thine heart is not with me? Thou hast mocked me these three times, and hast not told me wherein thy great strength lieth.

16 And it came to pass, when she pressed him daily with her words, and urged him, so that his soul was vexed unto death;

17 That he told her all his heart, and said unto her, There hath not come a razor upon mine head; for I have been a Nazarite unto God from my mother's womb: if I be shaven, then my strength will go from me, and I shall become weak, and be like any other man.

Author's comment

¹⁸ And when Delilah saw that he had told her all his heart, she sent and called for the lords of the Philistines, saying, Come up this once, for he hath shewed me all his heart. Then the lords of the Philistines came up unto her, and brought money in their hand.

¹⁹ And she made him sleep upon her knees; and she called for a man, and she caused him to shave off the seven locks of his head; and she began to afflict him, and his strength went from him.

²⁰ And she said, The Philistines be upon thee, Samson. And he awoke out of his sleep, and said, I will go out as at other times before, and shake myself. And he wist not that the LORD was departed from him.

²¹ But the Philistines took him, and put out his eyes, and brought him down to Gaza, and bound him with fetters of brass; and he did grind in the prison house.

²² Howbeit the hair of his head began to grow again after he was shaven.

SAMSON DIES WITH THE PHILISTINES

23 Then the lords of the Philistines gathered them together for to offer a great sacrifice unto Dagon their god, and to rejoice: for they said, Our god hath delivered Samson our enemy into our hand.

24 And when the people saw him, they praised their god: for they said, Our god hath delivered into our hands our enemy, and the destroyer of our country, which slew many of us.

25 And it came to pass, when their hearts were merry, that they said, Call for Samson, that he may make us sport. And they called for Samson out of the prison house; and he made them sport: and they set him between the pillars.

26 And Samson said unto the lad that held him by the hand; Suffer me that I may feel the pillars whereupon the house standeth, that I may lean upon them.

27 Now the house was full of men and women; and all the lords of the Philistines were there; and there were upon the roof about three thousand men and women that beheld while Samson made sport.

28 And Samson called unto the Lord, and said, O Lord God, remember me, I pray thee, and strengthen me, I pray thee, only this once, O

God, that I may be at once avenged of the Philistines for my two eyes.

29 And Samson took hold of the two middle pillars upon which the house stood, and on which it was borne up, of the one with his right hand, and of the other with his left.

30 And Samson said, Let me die with the Philistines. And he bowed himself with all his might; and the house fell upon the lords, and upon all the people that were therein. So the dead which he slew at his death were more than they which he slew in his life.31

Author's comment

The goal of the adversary and the Enticer's monetary benefit is not the end; God's accomplished mission is.

Episodic Conclusion

____

31JUDGES 16:1-30 KING JAMES VERSION (KJV)

Again the children of Israel did evil in the sight of the Lord, and the Lord delivered them into the hands of the Philistines for forty years. To deliver Israel, the Lord used Samson, who was born of a woman declared to be barren, with the instruction that his hair not ever to be shaved; but Delilah nagged Samson so much that he divulged this secret. She shaves off his hair; he loses his power, and is taken into captivity. His hair grows; he prays God, regains his strength, and is able to complete His assignment of decimating thousands of Philistines.

We have to stay focused and avoid the temptation of human frailty and being ensnared by deceit.

EPISODE 11: NAOMI, RUTH AND BOAZ

ELIMELECH'S FAMILY GOES TO MOAB

Now it came to pass in the days when the judges ruled, that there was a famine in the land. And a certain man of Bethlehemjudah went to sojourn in the country of Moab, he, and his wife, and his two sons.

2 And the name of the man was Elimelech, and the name of his wife Naomi, and the name of his two sons Mahlon and Chilion, Ephrathites of Bethlehemjudah. And they came into the country of Moab, and continued there.

3 And Elimelech Naomi's husband died; and she was left, and her two sons.

4 And they took them wives of the women of Moab; the name of the one was Orpah, and the name of the other Ruth: and they dwelled there about ten years.

5 And Mahlon and Chilion died also both of them; and the woman was left of her two sons and her husband.[32]

---

[32] Ruth 1:1-5 King James Version (KJV)

8 And Naomi said unto her two daughters in law, Go, return each to her mother's house:
the LORD deal kindly with you, as ye have dealt with the dead, and with me

9 The LORD grant you that ye may find rest, each of you in the house of her husband. Then she kissed them; and they lifted up their voice, and wept.

10 And they said unto her, surely we will return with thee unto thy people.

11 And Naomi said, Turn again, my daughters: why will ye go with me? Are there yet any more sons in my womb, that they may be your husbands?

12 Turn again, my daughters, go your way; for I am too old to have an husband. If I should say, I have hope, if I should have an husband also to night, and should also bear sons;

13 Would ye tarry for them till they were grown? Would ye stay for them from having husbands? Nay, my daughters; for it grieves me much for your sakes that the hand of the LORD is gone out against me.

14 And they lifted up their voice, and wept again: and Orpah kissed her mother in law; but Ruth clave unto her.

15 And she said, Behold, thy sister in law is gone back unto her people, and unto her gods: return thou after thy sister in law.

16 And Ruth said, Intreat me not to leave thee, or to return from following after thee: for whither thou goest, I will go; and where thou lodgest, I will lodge: thy people shall be my people, and thy God my God:

17 Where thou diest, will I die, and there will I be buried: the LORD do so to me, and more also, if ought but death part thee and me.

18 When she saw that she was steadfastly minded to go with her, then she left speaking unto her.

19 So they two went until they came to Bethlehem. And it came to pass, when they were come to Bethlehem, that all the city was moved about them, and they said, Is this Naomi?

20 And she said unto them, Call me not Naomi, call me Mara: for the Almighty hath dealt very bitterly with me.

21 I went out full and the LORD hath brought me home again empty: why then call ye me Naomi, seeing the LORD hath testified against me, and the Almighty hath afflicted me?

[22] So Naomi returned, and Ruth the Moabitess, her daughter in law, with her, which returned out of the country of Moab: and they came to Bethlehem in the beginning of barley harvest.[33]

RUTH MEETS BOAZ

And Naomi had a kinsman of her husband's, a mighty man of wealth, of the family of Elimelech; and his name was Boaz.

[2] And Ruth the Moabitess said unto Naomi Let me now go to the field, and glean ears of corn after him in whose sight I shall find grace. And she said unto her, Go, my daughter.

[3] And she went, and came, and gleaned in the field after the reapers: and her hap was to light on a part of the field belonging unto Boaz, who was of the kindred of Elimelech.

[4] And, behold, Boaz came from Bethlehem, and said unto the reapers, The LORD be with you. And they answered him, The LORD bless thee.

[5] Then said Boaz unto his servant that was set over the reapers, whose damsel is this?

[6] And the servant that was set over the reapers answered and said, it is the Moabites' damsel

---

that came back with Naomi out of the country of Moab:

7 And she said I pray you, let me glean and gather after the reapers among the sheaves: so she came, and hath continued even from the morning until now, that she tarried a little in the house.

8 Then said Boaz unto Ruth, Hearest thou not, my daughter? Go not to glean in another field, neither go from hence, but abide here fast by my maidens:

9 Let thine eyes be on the field that they do reap, and go thou after them: have I not charged the young men that they shall not touch thee? And when thou art athirst, go unto the vessels, and drink of that which the young men have drawn.

10 Then she fell on her face, and bowed herself to the ground, and said unto him, Why have I found grace in thine eyes, that thou shouldest take knowledge of me, seeing I am a stranger?

11 And Boaz answered and said unto her, It hath fully been shewed me, all that thou hast done unto thy mother in law since the death of thine husband: and how thou hast left thy father and thy mother, and the land of thy nativity, and art come unto a people which thou knewest not heretofore.

¹² The LORD recompense thy work, and a full reward be given thee of the LORD God of Israel, under whose wings thou art come to trust.

¹³ Then she said, Let me find favor in thy sight, my lord; for that thou hast comforted me, and for that thou hast spoken friendly unto thine handmaid, though I be not like unto one of thine handmaidens.

¹⁴ And Boaz said unto her, At mealtime come thou hither, and eat of the bread, and dip thy morsel in the vinegar. And she sat beside the reapers: and he reached her parched corn, and she did eat, and was sufficed, and left.

¹⁵ And when she was risen up to glean, Boaz commanded his young men, saying, Let her glean even among the sheaves, and reproach her not:

¹⁶ And let fall also some of the handfuls of purpose for her, and leave them, that she may glean them, and rebuke her not.

¹⁷ So she gleaned in the field until even, and beat out that she had gleaned: and it was about an ephah of barley.

¹⁸ And she took it up, and went into the city: and her mother in law saw what she had gleaned:

and she brought forth, and gave to her that she had reserved after she was sufficed.

¹⁹ And her mother in law said unto her, Where hast thou gleaned today? And where wroughtest thou? Blessed be he that did take knowledge of thee. And she shewed her mother in law with whom she had wrought, and said, The man's name with whom I wrought today is Boaz.

²⁰ And Naomi said unto her daughter in law, blessed be he of the LORD, who hath not left off his kindness to the living and to the dead. And Naomi said unto her, the man is near of kin unto us, one of our next kinsmen.

²¹ And Ruth the Moabitess said, He said unto me also, Thou shalt keep fast by my young men, until they have ended all my harvest.

²² And Naomi said unto Ruth her daughter in law, It is good, my daughter, that thou go out with his maidens, that they meet thee not in any other field.

²³ So she kept fast by the maidens of Boaz to glean unto the end of barley harvest and of wheat harvest; and dwelt with her mother in law.[34]

---

[34] Ruth 2:1-23 King James Version (KJV)

Then Naomi her mother in law said unto her, my daughter, shall I not seek rest for thee, that it may be well with thee?

2 And now is not Boaz of our kindred, with whose maidens thou wast? Behold, he winnoweth barley to night in the threshing floor.

3 Wash thyself therefore, and anoint thee, and put thy raiment upon thee, and get thee down to the floor: but make not thyself known unto the man, until he shall have done eating and drinking.

Author's comment

Women are Divine planners..

4 And it shall be, when he lieth down, that thou shalt mark the place where he shall lie, and thou shalt go in, and uncover his feet, and lay thee down; and he will tell thee what thou shalt do.

5 And she said unto her, All that thou sayest unto me I will do.

6 And she went down unto the floor, and did according to all that her mother in law bade her.

7 And when Boaz had eaten and drunk, and his heart was merry, he went to lie down at the end of the heap of corn: and she came softly, and uncovered his feet, and laid her down.

8 And it came to pass at midnight, that the man was afraid, and turned himself: and, behold, a woman lay at his feet.

9 And he said, Who art thou? And she answered, I am Ruth thine handmaid: spread therefore thy skirt over thine handmaid; for thou art a near kinsman.

10 And he said, Blessed be thou of the LORD, my daughter: for thou hast shewed more kindness in the latter end than at the beginning, inasmuch as thou followedst not young men, whether poor or rich.

11 And now, my daughter, fear not; I will do to thee all that thou requirest: for all the city of my people doth know that thou art a virtuous woman.

12 And now it is true that I am thy near kinsman: howbeit there is a kinsman nearer than I.

13 Tarry this night, and it shall be in the morning, that if he will perform unto thee the part of a kinsman, well; let him do the kinsman's part: but if he will not do the part of a

kinsman to thee, then will I do the part of a kinsman to thee, as the LORD liveth: lie down until the morning.

14 And she lay at his feet until the morning: and she rose up before one could know another. And he said; Let it not be known that a woman came into the floor.

15 Also he said, Bring the veil that thou hast upon thee, and hold it. And when she held it, he measured six measures of barley, and laid it on her: and she went into the city.

16 And when she came to her mother in law, she said, Who art thou, my daughter? And she told her all that the man had done to her.

17 And she said, these six measures of barley gave he me; for he said to me, Go not empty unto thy mother in law.

18 Then said she, Sit still, my daughter, until thou know how the matter will fall: for the man will not be in rest, until he have finished the thing this day.35

BOAZ REDEEMS RUTH: THE LORD BLESSES FAITHFULNESS WITH GOOD ROMANCE

---

35 RUTH 3:1-18 KING JAMES VERSION (KJV)

Then went Boaz up to the gate, and sat him down there: and, behold, the kinsman of whom Boaz spake came by; unto whom he said, Ho, such a one! turn aside, sit down here. And he turned aside, and sat down.

2 And he took ten men of the elders of the city, and said, Sit ye down here. And they sat down.

3 And he said unto the kinsman, Naomi that is come again out of the country of Moab, selleth a parcel of land, which was our brother Elimelech's:

4 And I thought to advertise thee, saying, Buy it before the inhabitants, and before the elders of my people. If thou wilt redeem it, redeem it: but if thou wilt not redeem it, then tell me, that I may know: for there is none to redeem it beside thee; and I am after thee. And he said, I will redeem it.

5 Then said Boaz, What day thou buyest the field of the hand of Naomi, thou must buy it also of Ruth the Moabitess, the wife of the dead, to raise up the name of the dead upon his inheritance.

6 And the kinsman said, I cannot redeem it for myself, lest I mar mine own inheritance: redeem thou my right to thyself; for I cannot redeem it.

7 Now this was the manner in former time in Israel concerning redeeming and concerning changing, for to confirm all things; a man plucked off his shoe, and gave it to his neighbor: and this was a testimony in Israel.

8 Therefore the kinsman said unto Boaz Buy it for thee. So he drew off his shoe.

9 And Boaz said unto the elders, and unto all the people, Ye are witnesses this day, that I have bought all that was Elimelech's, and all that was Chilion's and Mahlon's, of the hand of Naomi.

10 Moreover Ruth the Moabitess, the wife of Mahlon, have I purchased to be my wife, to raise up the name of the dead upon his inheritance, that the name of the dead be not cut off from among his brethren, and from the gate of his place: ye are witnesses this day.

11 And all the people that were in the gate, and the elders, said, We are witnesses.
The LORD make the woman that is come into thine house like Rachel and like Leah, which two did build the house of Israel: and do thou worthily in Ephratah, and be famous in Bethlehem:

12 And let thy house be like the house of Pharez, whom Tamar bare unto Judah, of the seed

which the LORD shall give thee of this young woman.

DESCENDANTS OF BOAZ AND RUTH

13 So Boaz took Ruth, and she was his wife: and when he went in unto her, the LORD gave her conception, and she bare a son.

14 And the women said unto Naomi, Blessed be the LORD, which hath not left thee this day without a kinsman, that his name may be famous in Israel.

15 And he shall be unto thee a restorer of thy life, and a nourisher of thine old age: for thy daughter in law, which loveth thee, which is better to thee than seven sons, hath born him.

16 And Naomi took the child, and laid it in her bosom, and became nurse unto it.

17 And the women her neighbors gave it a name, saying, There is a son born to Naomi; and they called his name Obed: he is the father of Jesse, the father of David.

18 Now these are the generations of Pharez: Pharez begat Hezron,

19 And Hezron begat Ram, and Ram begat Amminadab,

[20] And Amminadab begat Nahshon, and Nahshon begat Salmon,

[21] And Salmon begat Boaz, and Boaz begat Obed,

[22] And Obed begat Jesse and Jesse begat David.[36]

EPISODIC CONCLUSION

Because of famine in Canaan, Elimelech took his wife Naomi and two sons to sojourn in the country of Moab. Elimelech died. His sons married Moabite women, one of whom was called Ruth. The sons also died without children. Naomi determined to return to the country of her own people. She therefore released the girls to return to their mothers. Ruth refused to part with Naomi pledging to die where Naomi died and worship her God. The two returned to Canaan where Ruth was blessed with marriage to a rich man, Boaz, through kinsman redemption.

Ruth truly loved her widowed mother-in-law. She pledged to take care of her rather than worry about her own situation. She was blessed for her unselfishness.

---

[36] Ruth 4:1-22 King James Version (KJV)

Episode 12: Esther and Mordecai

The King Dethrones Queen Vashti

Now it came to pass in the days of Ahasuerus, (this is Ahasuerus which reigned, from India even unto Ethiopia, over an hundred and seven and twenty provinces :)

2 That in those days, when the king Ahasuerus sat on the throne of his kingdom, which was in Shushan the palace, 3

In the third year of his reign, he made a feast unto all his princes and his servants; the power of Persia and Media, the nobles and princes of the provinces, being before him:

4 When he shewed the riches of his glorious kingdom and the honor of his excellent majesty many days, even an hundred and fourscore days.

5 And when these days were expired, the king made a feast unto all the people that were present in Shushan the palace, both unto great and small, seven days, in the court of the garden of the king's palace;

6 Where were white, green, and blue, hangings, fastened with cords of fine linen and purple to

silver rings and pillars of marble: the beds were of gold and silver, upon a pavement of red, and blue, and white, and black, marble.

7 And they gave them drink in vessels of gold, (the vessels being diverse one from another,) and royal wine in abundance, according to the state of the king.

8 And the drinking was according to the law; none did compel: for so the king had appointed to all the officers of his house that they should do according to every man's pleasure.

9 Also Vashti the queen made a feast for the women in the royal house which belonged to king Ahasuerus.

10 On the seventh day, when the heart of the king was merry with wine, he commanded Mehuman, Biztha, Harbona, Bigtha, and Abagtha, Zethar, and Carcas, the seven chamberlains that served in the presence of Ahasuerus the king, 11 To bring Vashti the queen before the king with the crown royal, to shew the people and the princes her beauty: for she was fair to look on.

12 But the queen Vashti refused to come at the king's commandment by his chamberlains: therefore was the king very wroth, and his anger burned in him.

¹³ Then the king said to the wise men, which knew the times, (for so was the king's manner toward all that knew law and judgment:

¹⁴ And the next unto him was Carshena, Shethar, Admatha, Tarshish, Meres, Marsena, and Memucan, the seven princes of Persia and Media, which saw the king's face, and which sat the first in the kingdom;

¹⁵ What shall we do unto the queen Vashti according to law, because she hath not performed the commandment of the king Ahasuerus by the chamberlains?

¹⁶ And Memucan answered before the king and the princes, Vashti the queen hath not done wrong to the king only, but also to all the princes, and to all the people that are in all the provinces of the king Ahasuerus.

¹⁷ For this deed of the queen shall come abroad unto all women, so that they shall despise their husbands in their eyes, when it shall be reported, The king Ahasuerus commanded Vashti the queen to be brought in before him, but she came not.

¹⁸ Likewise shall the ladies of Persia and Media say this day unto all the king's princes, which have heard of the deed of the queen. Thus shall there arise too much contempt and wrath.

¹⁹ If it please the king, let there go a royal commandment from him, and let it be written among the laws of the Persians and the Medes, that it be not altered, That Vashti come no more before king Ahasuerus; and let the king give her royal estate unto another that is better than she.

²⁰ And when the king's decree which he shall make shall be published throughout all his empire, (for it is great,) all the wives shall give to their husbands honor both to great and small.

²¹ And the saying pleased the king and the princes; and the king did according to the word of Memucan:

²² For he sent letters into all the king's provinces, into every province according to the writing thereof, and to every people after their language, that every man should bear rule in his own house, and that it should be published according to the language of every people.[37]

ESTHER BECOMES QUEEN

After these things, when the wrath of king Ahasuerus was appeased, he remembered Vashti, and what she had done, and what was decreed against her.

----

[37] ESTHER 1:1-22 KING JAMES VERSION (KJV)

2 Then said the king's servants that ministered unto him, Let there be fair young virgins sought for the king:

3 And let the king appoint officers in all the provinces of his kingdom, that they may gather together all the fair young virgins unto Shushan the palace, to the house of the women, unto the custody of Hege the king's chamberlain, keeper of the women; and let their things for purification be given them:

4 And let the maiden which pleaseth the king be queen instead of Vashti. And the thing pleased the king; and he did so.

5 Now in Shushan the palace there was a certain Jew, whose name was Mordecai, the son of Jair, the son of Shimei, the son of Kish, a Benjamite;

6 Who had been carried away from Jerusalem with the captivity which had been carried away with Jeconiah king of Judah, whom Nebuchadnezzar the king of Babylon had carried away.

7 And he brought up Hadassah, that is, Esther, his uncle's daughter: for she had neither father nor mother, and the maid was fair and beautiful; whom Mordecai, when her father and mother were dead, took for his own daughter.

[8] So it came to pass, when the king's commandment and his decree was heard, and when many maidens were gathered together unto Shushan the palace, to the custody of Hegai, that Esther was brought also unto the king's house, to the custody of Hegai, keeper of the women.

[9] And the maiden pleased him, and she obtained kindness of him; and he speedily gave her things for purification, with such things as belonged to her, and seven maidens, which were meet to be given her, out of the king's house: and he preferred her and her maids unto the best place of the house of the women.

[10] Esther had not shewed her people nor her kindred: for Mordecai had charged her that she should not shew it.

[11] And Mordecai walked every day before the court of the women's house, to know how Esther did, and what should become of her.

[12] Now when every maid's turn was come to go in to king Ahasuerus, after that she had been twelve months, according to the manner of the women, (for so were the days of their purifications accomplished, to wit, six months with oil of myrrh, and six months with sweet odors, and with other things for the purifying of the women;)

13 Then thus came every maiden unto the king; whatsoever she desired was given her to go with her out of the house of the women unto the king's house.

14 In the evening she went, and on the morrow she returned into the second house of the women, to the custody of Shaashgaz, the king's chamberlain, which kept the concubines: she came in unto the king no more, except the king delighted in her, and that she were called by name.

15 Now when the turn of Esther, the daughter of Abihail the uncle of Mordecai, who had taken her for his daughter, was come to go in unto the king, she required nothing but what Hegai the king's chamberlain, the keeper of the women, appointed. And Esther obtained favor in the sight of all them that looked upon her.

Author's comment

Like Eve, Esther was sublimely crafted.

16 So Esther was taken unto king Ahasuerus into his house royal in the tenth month, which is the month Tebeth, in the seventh year of his reign.

17 And the king loved Esther above all the women, and she obtained grace and favor in his

sight more than all the virgins; so that he set the royal crown upon her head, and made her queen instead of Vashti.

18 Then the king made a great feast unto all his princes and his servants, even Esther's feast; and he made a release to the provinces, and gave gifts, according to the state of the king.

MORDECAI DISCOVERS A PLOT

19 And when the virgins were gathered together the second time, then Mordecai sat in the king's gate.

20 Esther had not yet shewed her kindred nor her people; as Mordecai had charged her: for Esther did the commandment of Mordecai, like as when she was brought up with him.

21 In those days, while Mordecai sat in the king's gate, two of the king's chamberlains, Bigthan and Teresh, of those which kept the door, were wroth, and sought to lay hands on the king Ahasuerus.

22 And the thing was known to Mordecai, who told it unto Esther the queen; and Esther certified the king thereof in Mordecai's name.

23 And when inquisition was made of the matter, it was found out; therefore they were both

hanged on a tree: and it was written in the book of the chronicles before the king.[38]

HAMAN'S CONSPIRACY AGAINST THE JEWS

After these things did king Ahasuerus promote Haman the son of Hammedatha the Agagite, and advanced him, and set his seat above all the princes that were with him.

[2] And all the king's servants, that were in the king's gate, bowed, and reverenced Haman: for the king had so commanded concerning him. But Mordecai bowed not, nor did him reverence.

[3] Then the king's servants, which were in the king's gate, said unto Mordecai, Why transgressest thou the king's commandment?

[4] Now it came to pass, when they spake daily unto him, and he hearkened not unto them, that they told Haman, to see whether Mordecai's matters would stand: for he had told them that he was a Jew.

[5] And when Haman saw that Mordecai bowed not, nor did him reverence, then was Haman full of wrath.

---

[38] ESTHER 2:1-23 KING JAMES VERSION (KJV)

⁶ And he thought scorn to lay hands on Mordecai alone; for they had shewed him the people of Mordecai: wherefore Haman sought to destroy all the Jews that were throughout the whole kingdom of Ahasuerus, even the people of Mordecai.

⁷ In the first month, that is, the month Nisan, in the twelfth year of king Ahasuerus, they cast Pur, that is, the lot, before Haman from day to day, and from month to month, to the twelfth month, that is, the month Adar.

⁸ And Haman said unto king Ahasuerus, There is a certain people scattered abroad and dispersed among the people in all the provinces of thy kingdom; and their laws are diverse from all people; neither keep they the king's laws: therefore it is not for the king's profit to suffer them.

⁹ If it please the king, let it be written that they may be destroyed: and I will pay ten thousand talents of silver to the hands of those that have the charge of the business, to bring it into the king's treasuries.

¹⁰ And the king took his ring from his hand, and gave it unto Haman the son of Hammedatha the Agagite, the Jews' enemy.

11 And the king said unto Haman, The silver is given to thee, the people also, to do with them as it seemeth good to thee.

12 Then were the king's scribes called on the thirteenth day of the first month, and there was written according to all that Haman had commanded unto the king's lieutenants, and to the governors that were over every province, and to the rulers of every people of every province according to the writing thereof, and to every people after their language; in the name of king Ahasuerus was it written, and sealed with the king's ring.

13 And the letters were sent by posts into all the king's provinces, to destroy, to kill, and to cause to perish, all Jews, both young and old, little children and women, in one day, even upon the thirteenth day of the twelfth month, which is the month Adar, and to take the spoil of them for a prey.

14 The copy of the writing for a commandment to be given in every province was published unto all people, that they should be ready against that day.

15 The posts went out, being hastened by the king's commandment, and the decree was given in Shushan the palace. And the king and Haman

sat down to drink; but the city Shushan was perplexed.[39]

ESTHER AGREES TO HELP THE JEWS

When Mordecai perceived all that was done, Mordecai rent his clothes, and put on sackcloth with ashes, and went out into the midst of the city, and cried with a loud and a bitter cry;

2 And came even before the king's gate: for none might enter into the king's gate clothed with sackcloth.

3 And in every province, whithersoever the king's commandment and his decree came, there was great mourning among the Jews, and fasting, and weeping, and wailing; and many lay in sackcloth and ashes.

4 So Esther's maids and her chamberlains came and told it her. Then was the queen exceedingly grieved; and she sent raiment to clothe Mordecai, and to take away his sackcloth from him: but he received it not.

5 Then called Esther for Hatach, one of the king's chamberlains, whom he had appointed to attend upon her, and gave him a commandment to Mordecai, to know what it was, and why it was.

---

[39] Esther 3:1-15 King James Version (KJV)

6 So Hatach went forth to Mordecai unto the street of the city, which was before the king's gate.

7 And Mordecai told him of all that had happened unto him, and of the sum of the money that Haman had promised to pay to the king's treasuries for the Jews, to destroy them.

8 Also he gave him the copy of the writing of the decree that was given at Shushan to destroy them, to shew it unto Esther, and to declare it unto her, and to charge her that she should go in unto the king, to make supplication unto him, and to make request before him for her people.

9 And Hatach came and told Esther the words of Mordecai.

10 Again Esther spake unto Hatach, and gave him commandment unto Mordecai;

11 All the king's servants, and the people of the king's provinces, do know, that whosoever, whether man or women, shall come unto the king into the inner court, who is not called, there is one law of his to put him to death, except such to whom the king shall hold out the golden scepter, that he may live: but I have not been called to come in unto the king these thirty days.

¹² And they told to Mordecai Esther's words.

¹³ Then Mordecai commanded to answer Esther, Think not with thyself that thou shalt escape in the king's house, more than all the Jews.

¹⁴ For if thou altogether holdest thy peace at this time, then shall there enlargement and deliverance arise to the Jews from another place; but thou and thy father's house shall be destroyed: and who knoweth whether thou art come to the kingdom for such a time as this?

¹⁵ Then Esther bade them return Mordecai this answer,

¹⁶ Go, gather together all the Jews that are present in Shushan, and fast ye for me, and neither eat nor drink three days, night or day: I also and my maidens will fast likewise; and so will I go in unto the king, which is not according to the law: and if I perish, I perish. ¹⁷ So Mordecai went his way, and did according to all that Esther had commanded him.[40]

ESTHER'S BANQUET

Now it came to pass on the third day that Esther put on her royal apparel, and stood in the inner court of the king's house, over against the king's house: and the king sat upon his royal throne in

---

[40] Esther 4:1-17 King James Version (KJV)

the royal house, over against the gate of the house.

2 And it was so, when the king saw Esther the queen standing in the court, that she obtained favor in his sight: and the king held out to Esther the golden scepter that was in his hand. So Esther drew near, and touched the top of the scepter.

3 Then said the king unto her, What wilt thou, Queen Esther? and what is thy request? it shall be even given thee to the half of the kingdom. 4 And Esther answered, If it seem good unto the king, let the king and Haman come this day unto the banquet that I have prepared for him.

5 Then the king said, Cause Haman to make haste that he may do as Esther hath said. So the king and Haman came to the banquet that Esther had prepared.

6 And the king said unto Esther at the banquet of wine, What is thy petition? and it shall be granted thee: and what is thy request? Even to the half of the kingdom it shall be performed.

7 Then answered Esther, and said, my petition and my request is;

8 If I have found favor in the sight of the king, and if it please the king to grant my petition, and to perform my request, let the king and Haman come to the banquet that I shall prepare for them, and I will do tomorrow as the king hath said.

HAMAN'S PLOT AGAINST MORDECAI

9 Then went Haman forth that day joyful and with a glad heart: but when Haman saw Mordecai in the king's gate, that he stood not up, nor moved for him, he was full of indignation against Mordecai.

10 Nevertheless Haman refrained himself: and when he came home, he sent and called for his friends and Zeresh his wife.

11 And Haman told them of the glory of his riches, and the multitude of his children, and all the things wherein the king had promoted him, and how he had advanced him above the princes and servants of the king.

12 Haman said moreover, Yea, Esther the queen did let no man come in with the king unto the

banquet that she had prepared but myself; and tomorrow am I invited unto her also with the king.

13 Yet all this availeth me nothing, so long as I see Mordecai the Jew sitting at the king's gate.

14 Then said Zeresh his wife and all his friends unto him, Let a gallows be made of fifty cubits high, and tomorrow speak thou unto the king that Mordecai may be hanged thereon: then go thou in merrily with the king unto the banquet. And the thing pleased Haman; and he caused the gallows to be made.41

THE KING HONORS MORDECAI

On that night could not the king sleep, and he commanded to bring the book of records of the chronicles; and they were read before the king.

2 And it was found written, that Mordecai had told of Bigthana and Teresh, two of the king's chamberlains, the keepers of the door, who sought to lay hand on the king Ahasuerus.

3 And the king said, What honor and dignity hath been done to Mordecai for this? Then said the king's servants that ministered unto him, There is nothing done for him.

---

41 ESTHER 5:1-14 KING JAMES VERSION (KJV)

4 And the king said who is in the court? Now Haman was come into the outward court of the king's house, to speak unto the king to hang Mordecai on the gallows that he had prepared for him.

5 And the king's servants said unto him, Behold, Haman standeth in the court. And the king said, Let him come in.

6 So Haman came in. And the king said unto him, what shall be done unto the man whom the king delighteth to honor? Now Haman thought in his heart, To whom would the king delight to do honor more than to myself?

7 And Haman answered the king, For the man whom the king delighteth to honor, 8 Let the royal apparel be brought which the king useth to wear, and the horse that the king rideth upon, and the crown royal which is set upon his head:

9 And let this apparel and horse be delivered to the hand of one of the king's most noble princes, that they may array the man withal whom the king delighteth to honor, and bring him on horseback through the street of the city, and proclaim before him, Thus shall it be done to the man whom the king delighteth to honor.

¹⁰ Then the king said to Haman, Make haste, and take the apparel and the horse, as thou hast said, and do even so to Mordecai the Jew, that sitteth at the king's gate: let nothing fail of all that thou hast spoken.

¹¹ Then took Haman the apparel and the horse, and arrayed Mordecai, and brought him on horseback through the street of the city, and proclaimed before him, Thus shall it be done unto the man whom the king delighteth to honor.

¹² And Mordecai came again to the king's gate. But Haman hasted to his house mourning, and having his head covered.

¹³ And Haman told Zeresh his wife and all his friends everything that had befallen him. Then said his wise men and Zeresh his wife unto him, If Mordecai be of the seed of the Jews, before whom thou hast begun to fall, thou shalt not prevail against him, but shalt surely fall before him.

¹⁴ And while they were yet talking with him, came the king's chamberlains, and hasted to bring Haman unto the banquet that Esther had prepared.[42]

HAMAN HANGED INSTEAD OF MORDECAI

---

[42] Esther 6:1-14 King James Version (KJV)

So the king and Haman came to banquet with Esther the queen.

2 And the king said again unto Esther on the second day at the banquet of wine, what is thy petition, Queen Esther? And it shall be granted thee: and what is thy request? And it shall be performed, even to the half of the kingdom.

3 Then Esther the queen answered and said, If I have found favor in thy sight, O king, and if it please the king, let my life be given me at my petition, and my people at my request:

4 For we are sold, I and my people, to be destroyed, to be slain, and to perish. But if we had been sold for bondmen and bondwomen, I had held my tongue, although the enemy could not countervail the king's damage.

5 Then the king Ahasuerus answered and said unto Esther the queen, who is he, and where is he, that durst presume in his heart to do so?

6 And Esther said, the adversary and enemy is this wicked Haman. Then Haman was afraid before the king and the queen.

7 And the king arising from the banquet of wine in his wrath went into the palace garden: and Haman stood up to make request for his life to

Esther the queen; for he saw that there was evil determined against him by the king.

8 Then the king returned out of the palace garden into the place of the banquet of wine; and Haman was fallen upon the bed whereon Esther was. Then said the king, Will he force the queen also before me in the house? As the word went out of king's mouth, they covered Haman's face.

9 And Harbonah, one of the chamberlains, said before the king, Behold also, the gallows fifty cubits high, which Haman had made for Mordecai, who spoken good for the king, standeth in the house of Haman. Then the king said, Hang him thereon.

10 So they hanged Haman on the gallows that he had prepared for Mordecai. Then was the king's wrath pacified.[43]

ESTHER SAVES THE JEWS

On that day did the king Ahasuerus give the house of Haman the Jews' enemy unto Esther the queen. And Mordecai came before the king; for Esther had told what he was unto her.

2 And the king took off his ring, which he had taken from Haman, and gave it unto Mordecai.

---

[43] Esther 7:1-10 King James Version (KJV)

And Esther set Mordecai over the house of
Haman.

3 And Esther spake yet again before the king and
fell down at his feet, and besought him with
tears to put away the mischief of Haman the
Agagite, and his device that he had devised
against the Jews.

4 Then the king held out the golden scepter
toward Esther. So Esther arose, and stood
before the king,

5 And said, If it please the king, and if I have
favor in his sight, and the thing seem right
before the king, and I be pleasing in his eyes, let
it be written to reverse the letters devised by
Haman the son of Hammedatha the Agagite,
which he wrote to destroy the Jews which are in
all the king's provinces:

6 For how can I endure to see the evil that shall
come unto my people? or how can I endure to
see the destruction of my kindred?

7 Then the king Ahasuerus said unto Esther the
queen and to Mordecai the Jew, Behold, I have
given Esther the house of Haman, and him they
have hanged upon the gallows, because he laid
his hand upon the Jews.

8 Write ye also for the Jews, as it liketh you, in the king's name, and seal it with the king's ring: for the writing which is written in the king's name, and sealed with the king's ring, may no man reverse.

9 Then were the king's scribes called at that time in the third month, that is, the month Sivan, on the three and twentieth day thereof; and it was written according to all that Mordecai commanded unto the Jews, and to the lieutenants, and the deputies and rulers of the provinces which are from India unto Ethiopia, an hundred twenty and seven provinces, unto every province according to the writing thereof, and unto every people after their language, and to the Jews according to their writing, and according to their language.

10 And he wrote in the king Ahasuerus' name, and sealed it with the king's ring, and sent letters by posts on horseback, and riders on mules, camels, and young dromedaries:

11 Wherein the king granted the Jews which were in every city to gather themselves together, and to stand for their life, to destroy, to slay and to cause to perish, all the power of the people and province that would assault them, both little ones and women, and to take the spoil of them for a prey,

[12] Upon one day in all the provinces of king Ahasuerus, namely, upon the thirteenth day of the twelfth month, which is the month Adar.

[13] The copy of the writing for a commandment to be given in every province was published unto all people, and that the Jews should be ready against that day to avenge themselves on their enemies.

[14] So the posts that rode upon mules and camels went out, being hastened and pressed on by the king's commandment. And the decree was given at Shushan the palace.

[15] And Mordecai went out from the presence of the king in royal apparel of blue and white, and with a great crown of gold, and with a garment of fine linen and purple: and the city of Shushan rejoiced and was glad.

[16] The Jews had light, and gladness, and joy, and honour.

[17] And in every province, and in every city, whithersoever the king's commandment and his decree came; the Jews had joy and gladness, a feast and a good day. And many of the people of the land became Jews; for the fear of the Jews fell upon them.[44]

---

[44] ESTHER 8:1-17 KING JAMES VERSION (KJV)

Now in the twelfth month, that is, the month Adar, on the thirteenth day of the same, when the king's commandment and his decree drew near to be put in execution, in the day that the enemies of the Jews hoped to have power over them, (though it was turned to the contrary, that the Jews had rule over them that hated them;)

2 The Jews gathered themselves together in their cities throughout all the provinces of the king Ahasuerus, to lay hand on such as sought their hurt: and no man could withstand them; for the fear of them fell upon all people.

3 And all the rulers of the provinces, and the lieutenants, and the deputies, and officers of the king, helped the Jews; because the fear of Mordecai fell upon them.

4 For Mordecai was great in the king's house, and his fame went out throughout all the provinces: for this man Mordecai waxed greater and greater.

5 Thus the Jews smote all their enemies with the stroke of the sword, and slaughter, and destruction, and did what they would unto those that hated them.

⁶ And in Shushan the palace the Jews slew and destroyed five hundred men.

⁷ And Parshandatha, and Dalphon, and Aspatha,

⁸ And Poratha, and Adalia, and Aridatha,

⁹ And Parmashta, and Arisai, and Aridai, and Vajezatha,

¹⁰ The ten sons of Haman the son of Hammedatha, the enemy of the Jews, slew them; but on the spoil laid they not their hand.

¹¹ On that day the number of those that were slain in Shushan the palace was brought before the king.

¹² And the king said unto Esther the queen, The Jews have slain and destroyed five hundred men in Shushan the palace, and the ten sons of Haman; what have they done in the rest of the king's provinces? Now what is thy petition? And it shall be granted thee: or what is thy request further? And it shall be done.

¹³ Then said Esther, If it please the king, let it be granted to the Jews which are in Shushan to do to morrow also according unto this day's decree, and let Haman's ten sons be hanged upon the gallows.

[14] And the king commanded it so to be done: and the decree was given at Shushan; and they hanged Haman's ten sons.

[15] For the Jews that were in Shushan gathered themselves together on the fourteenth day also of the month Adar, and slew three hundred men at Shushan; but on the prey they laid not their hand.[45]

EPISODIC CONCLUSION
Queen Vashti disobeys the instruction by King Ahueserus and loses her status as queen. By God's Grace, this creates the opportunity for a Jewish girl, Esther, to be selected by the king as the queen. Being Queen sets her up to be able to free the children of Israel.

Blessed are the meek for they shall inherit the earth. God blessed Esther super-abundantly. In turn, with the assistance of her cousin Mordecai she blessed the Israelites with freedom from extermination

---

[45] ESTHER 9:1-15 KING JAMES VERSION (KJV)

EPISODE 13: (TWO PARTNERSHIPS INTERTWINED): (I) MARY THE HIGHLY FAVORED AND JOSEPH THE OBEDIENT, AND :(II) ZACHARIAS AND ELI ZABETH THE RIGHTEOUS COUPLE

THE GENEALOGY OF JESUS CHRIST

2 Abraham begat Isaac; and Isaac begat Jacob; and Jacob begat Judas and his brethren;

3 And Judas begat Phares and Zara of Tamar; and Phares begat Esrom; and Esrom begat Aram;

4 And Aram begat Aminadab; and Aminadab begat Naasson; and Naasson begat Salmon;

5 And Salmon begat Booz of Rachab; and Booz begat Obed of Ruth; and Obed begat Jesse;

6 And Jesse begat David the king; and David the king begat Solomon of her that had been the wife of Uriah;

7 And Solomon begat Roboam; and Roboam begat Abia; and Abia begat Asa;

8 And Asa begat Josaphat; and Josaphat begat Joram; and Joram begat Ozias;

9 And Ozias begat Joatham; and Joatham begat Achaz; and Achaz begat Ezekias;

10 And Ezekias begat Manasses; and Manasses begat Amon; and Amon begat Josias;

11 And Josias begat Jechonias and his brethren, about the time they were carried away to Babylon:

12 And after they were brought to Babylon, Jechonias begat Salathiel; and Salathiel begat Zorobabel;

13 And Zorobabel begat Abiud; and Abiud begat Eliakim; and Eliakim begat Azor;

14 And Azor begat Sadoc; and Sadoc begat Achim; and Achim begat Eliud;

15 And Eliud begat Eleazar; and Eleazar begat Matthan; and Matthan begat Jacob;

16 And Jacob begat Joseph the husband of Mary, of whom was born Jesus, who is called Christ.[46]

---

[46] MATTHEW 1:1-16 KING JAMES VERSION (KJV)

⁵ There was in the days of Herod, the king of Judaea, a certain priest named Zacharias, of the course of Abia: and his wife was of the daughters of Aaron, and her name was Elisabeth.

⁶ And they were both righteous before God, walking in all the commandments and ordinances of the Lord blameless.

⁷ And they had no child, because that Elisabeth was barren, and they both were now well stricken in years.

⁸ And it came to pass, that while he executed the priest's office before God in the order of his course,

⁹ According to the custom of the priest's office, his lot was to burn incense when he went into the temple of the Lord.

¹⁰ And the whole multitude of the people were praying without at the time of incense.

11 And there appeared unto him an angel of the
Lord standing on the right side of the altar of
incense.

12 And when Zacharias saw him, he was
troubled, and fear fell upon him.

13 But the angel said unto him, Fear not,
Zacharias: for thy prayer is heard; and thy wife
Elisabeth shall bear thee a son, and thou shalt
call his name John.

Author's comment

*Again, the Lord unlocks the womb of a barren
and old woman and the result is greatness.*

14 And thou shalt have joy and gladness; and
many shall rejoice at his birth.

15 For he shall be great in the sight of the Lord,
and shall drink neither wine nor strong drink;
and he shall be filled with the Holy Ghost, even
from his mother's womb.

16 And many of the children of Israel shall he
turn to the Lord their God.

17 And he shall go before him in the spirit and
power of Elias, to turn the hearts of the fathers
to the children, and the disobedient to the
wisdom of the just; to make ready a people
prepared for the Lord.

¹⁸ And Zacharias said unto the angel, whereby shall I know this? for I am an old man, and my wife well stricken in years.

¹⁹ And the angel answering said unto him, I am Gabriel that stand in the presence of God; and am sent to speak unto thee and to shew thee these glad tidings.

²⁰ And, behold, thou shalt be dumb, and not able to speak, until the day that these things shall be performed, because thou believest not my words, which shall be fulfilled in their season.

²¹ And the people waited for Zacharias, and marveled that he tarried so long in the temple.

²² And when he came out, he could not speak unto them: and they perceived that he had seen a vision in the temple: for he beckoned unto them, and remained speechless.

²³ And it came to pass, that, as soon as the days of his ministration were accomplished, he departed to his own house.

²⁴ And after those days his wife Elisabeth conceived, and hid herself five months, saying,

²⁵ Thus hath the Lord dealt with me in the days wherein he looked on me, to take away my reproach among men.

26 And in the sixth month the angel Gabriel was sent from God unto a city of Galilee, named Nazareth,

27 To a virgin espoused to a man whose name was Joseph, of the house of David; and the virgin's name was Mary.

28 And the angel came in unto her, and said, Hail, thou that art highly favored, the Lord is with thee: blessed art thou among women.

29 And when she saw him, she was troubled at his saying, and cast in her mind what manner of salutation this should be.

30 And the angel said unto her, Fear not, Mary: for thou hast found favor with God.

31 And, behold, thou shalt conceive in thy womb, and bring forth a son, and shalt call his name JESUS.

Author's comment

God revealed to Rebekah that the roles of Esau and Jacob were going to be changed whilst Isaac remained ignorant. Likewise, the Angel Gabriel

³² He shall be great, and shall be called the Son of the Highest: and the Lord God shall give unto him the throne of his father David:

³³ And he shall reign over the house of Jacob for ever; and of his kingdom there shall be no end.

³⁴ Then said Mary unto the angel, How shall this be, seeing I know not a man?

³⁵ And the angel answered and said unto her, The Holy Ghost shall come upon thee, and the power of the Highest shall overshadow thee:

Therefore also that holy thing which shall be born of thee shall be called the Son of God.

³⁶ And, behold, thy cousin Elisabeth, she hath also conceived a son in her old age: and this is the sixth month with her, who was called barren.

³⁷ For with God nothing shall be impossible.

³⁸ And Mary said, Behold the handmaid of the Lord; be it unto me according to thy word. And the angel departed from her.

MARY VISITS ELIZABETH

³⁹ And Mary arose in those days, and went into the hill country with haste, into a city of Judah;

⁴⁰ And entered into the house of Zacharias, and saluted Elisabeth.

⁴¹ And it came to pass, that, when Elisabeth heard the salutation of Mary, the babe leaped in her womb; and Elisabeth was filled with the Holy Ghost:

⁴² And she spake out with a loud voice, and said, Blessed art thou among women, and blessed is the fruit of thy womb.

Author's comment

This is the only time in recorded history that this Holy Communication took place between Jesus in Mary's womb, and John in Elisabeth's womb-the one and only inter-uterine communication. What could Jesus have said to John? He might have said: "Go on ahead of Me, and tell them I preceded you".

⁴³ And whence is this to me that the mother of my Lord should come to me?

⁴⁴ For, lo, as soon as the voice of thy salutation sounded in mine ears, the babe leaped in my womb for joy.

⁴⁵ And blessed is she that believed: for there shall be a performance of those things which were told her from the Lord.

THE SONG OF MARY

⁴⁶ And Mary said, My soul doth magnify the Lord,

⁴⁷ And my spirit hath rejoiced in God my Savior.

⁴⁸ For he hath regarded the low estate of his handmaiden: for, behold, from henceforth all generations shall call me blessed.

⁴⁹ For he that is mighty hath done to me great things; and holy is his name.

⁵⁰ And his mercy is on them that fear him from generation to generation.

⁵¹ He hath shewed strength with his arm; he hath scattered the proud in the imagination of their hearts.

⁵² He hath put down the mighty from their seats, and exalted them of low degree.

⁵³ He hath filled the hungry with good things; and the rich he hath sent empty away.

⁵⁴ He hath helped his servant Israel, in remembrance of his mercy;

⁵⁵ As he spake to our fathers, to Abraham, and to his seed for ever.

⁵⁶ And Mary abode with her about three months, and returned to her own house.

BIRTH OF JOHN THE BAPTIST

⁵⁷ Now Elisabeth's full time came that she should be delivered; and she brought forth a son.

⁵⁸ And her neighbors and her cousins heard how the Lord had shewed great mercy upon her; and they rejoiced with her.

CIRCUMCISION OF JOHN THE BAPTIST

⁵⁹ And it came to pass, that on the eighth day they came to circumcise the child; and they called him Zacharias, after the name of his father.

⁶⁰ And his mother answered and said, Not so; but he shall be called John.

⁶¹ And they said unto her, There is none of thy kindred that is called by this name.

⁶² And they made signs to his father, how he would have him called.

⁶³ And he asked for a writing table, and wrote, saying, His name is John. And they marveled all.⁴⁷

CHRIST BORN OF MARY

¹⁸ Now the birth of Jesus Christ was on this wise: When as his mother Mary was espoused to Joseph, before they came together, she was found with child of the Holy Ghost.

¹⁹ Then Joseph her husband, being a just man, and not willing to make her a public example, was minded to put her away privily.

²⁰ But while he thought on these things, behold, the angel of the LORD appeared unto him in a dream, saying, Joseph, thou son of David, fear not to take unto thee Mary thy wife: for that which is conceived in her is of the Holy Ghost.

²¹ And she shall bring forth a son, and thou shalt call his name JESUS: for he shall save his people from their sins.

²² Now all this was done, that it might be fulfilled which was spoken of the Lord by the prophet, saying,

---

⁴⁷ LUKE 1:5-63 KING JAMES VERSION (KJV)

23 Behold, a virgin shall be with child, and shall bring forth a son, and they shall call his name Emmanuel, which being interpreted is, God with us.

24 Then Joseph being raised from sleep did as the angel of the Lord had bidden him, and took unto him his wife: OBEDIENCE![48]

And it came to pass in those days, that there went out a decree from Caesar Augustus that all the world should be taxed.

2 (And this taxing was first made when Cyrenius was governor of Syria.)

3 And all went to be taxed every one into his own city.

4 And Joseph also went up from Galilee, out of the city of Nazareth, into Judaea, unto the city of David, which is called Bethlehem; (because he was of the house and lineage of David :)

5 To be taxed with Mary his espoused wife, being great with child.

---

[48] MATTHEW 1:18-24 KING JAMES VERSION (KJV)

⁶ And so it was, that, while they were there, the days were accomplished that she should be delivered.

⁷ And she brought forth her firstborn son, and wrapped him in swaddling clothes, and laid him in a manger; because there was no room for them in the inn. THIS SIGNIFIES HUMILITY.[49]

Author's comment

During this sojourn He exercised such influence as to last mankind the whole eternity.

EPISODIC CONCLUSION

After Mary was engaged to Joseph, before they had sex, she was found with child of the Holy Spirit. Then Joseph her husband, being a just man, and not wanting to make her a public spectacle, thought of ending the affair secretly. But while he thought about these things, an angel of the Lord appeared to him in a dream, saying, "Joseph, son of David, do not be afraid to take to you Mary your wife, for that which is conceived in her is of the Holy Spirit. And she will bring forth a Son, and you

---

[49] LUKE 2:1-7 KING JAMES VERSION (KJV)

shall call His name JESUS, for He will save His people from their sins." Joseph obeyed.

This shows obedience, through faith, by Joseph. It also shows the immense love that God demonstrates to man by introducing His Son Jesus in the most humble of circumstances. Had God so wanted, He could have introduced Jesus in majestic circumstances and pomp. But He did not; because the things of this world are transient; and Jesus did not sacrifice His heavenly splendor for fleeting moments. He came to bring us the Good News of life eternal. Because of their righteousness, Zacharias and Elizabeth were blessed in their old age with the birth of a son, John the Baptist.

LESSONS LEARNT

ADAM AND EVE
This episode of the partnership of Adam and Eve demonstrates God's preparedness and ability to be the Super Planner and Provider of abundance. In Jeremiah 29:11, The Lord says this:

For I know the plans I have for you.

God is so thorough in planning our lives that He creates Adam and builds a state of the art luxury Garden of Eden for Adam's residence. Then God perceives that Adam needs company; He therefore made a woman and brought her to Adam. Through Eve the course of events was changed and they were expelled from Eden.

The thought that ought to inspire us is this: if God could do this much for Adam who was as yet not tested and still had a propensity to sin, how much more will He do for us believers in Christ? The Glory of Heaven is surely greater than the luxury of the Garden of Eden.

ABRAHAM, SARAH AND THEIR BOND-WOMAN HAGAR
God's power of creation: if God could create Adam out of the dust, getting 90 years old Sarah

to conceive Isaac was "child's play". After all, He had already created Eve out of Adam's rib.

And so, God delivered, on schedule, according to His promise despite Sarah's impatience and lack of confidence that caused her to instruct Abraham to sleep with Hagar. This instruction led to the formation of two distinct and inharmonious nations- Israel's and Ishmael's descendants.

Was it surprising to God? Hardly, it was rather His plan to ensure the purity and blessing of Israel and the multiplication of the descendants of Ishmael.

THE DESTRUCTION OF SODOM AND THE CONSEQUENT PARTNERSHIP OF LOT AND HIS DAUGHTERS
God also recreates after cleansing. He cleansed Sodom and Gomorrah through fire and brimstone leaving only Lot and his two daughters. God enacted His promise to bless Lot as He had made it to Abraham. Through this partnership of Lot and her daughters, they assured continuation of their father's family.

REBEKAH AND HER SON JACOB

Isaac loved his eldest son Esau, but Rebekah loved Jacob. While Isaac in his old age was planning to bless Esau, Rachel maneuvered to have Jacob receive the blessing. Was this treachery? At face value it is. However, Esau had previously sold his birthright to Jacob for a bowl of soup, in effect exchanging God's blessing for soup! This suggests that Esau did not have this burning desire for leadership; Jacob, on the other hand, had it. He had actually negotiated this leadership- for soup batter. It would be years later that the Son of God would enlighten the world by rebuking Satan with the words: *It is written, that man shall not live by bread alone, but by every word of God.*

THE PARTNERSHIPS OF JACOB'S SONS: REUBEN AND HIS STEP-MOTHER BILHAH; AND, JUDAH AND HIS DAUGHTER-IN-LAW TAMAR

Because of his illicit partnership with his father's concubine, Reuben lost the blessing of excellence that he should have enjoyed as a birthright. On the other hand, the unexpected union of Judah and his daughter-in-law brought us a great heredity including King David, and the Joseph of the Blessed Mary.

By the Grace of God, the good shall always triumph over evil. Therefore, despite the power of Ahab's throne and the extraordinarily powerful demonic spirit in Jezebel, God empowered Elijah in performing the miracle of fire for the burnt offering; slaughtering 450 Baal prophets; and, prophesying the end of the draught

ELIJAH AND THE WIDOW

As God the Father would later resurrect God the Son, God the Father restores life to the widow's son and she is filled with Belief.

SAMSON AND DELILAH

God works in astonishing ways. He will use people that to us are of questionable morals, to achieve His goals. Samson was appointed by God to decimate the Philistines; while Delilah was appointed by the Philistine lords to impede God's plan by afflicting Samson. Samson and Delilah had a common tool to discharge their appointments: sex. He used Samson's sex fanaticism and combined it with Delilah's attributes of a prostitute *(she was promised a bundle of money if she betrayed Samson)* to achieve His mission.

So, despite enticement being an effective tool of the devil, when Satan thinks he has conquered God's messenger, Samson, he ends up killing thousands of His people's enemies.

NAOMI, RUTH AND BOAZ

The story of Naomi, Ruth and Boaz is the story of righteousness and virtuosity in the face of trials. Persevering in goodness and selfless love touches God Almighty to bless the righteous.

ESTHER AND MORDECAI

Millennia passed after Esther and Mordecai, and it was time, in the New Testament, that Jesus the Son of God would declare: *Blessed are the meek; for they shall inherit the earth.*

Indeed the meekness of Esther, the Jewish girl earned her the inheritance, by God's Grace, forsaken by Queen Vashti through her arrogance and disrespect of King Ahasuerus. Moreover, Mordecai the meek seeker of righteousness inherited the powerful position of Haman whose arrogance and wickedness to God's people caused him to be hanged on the gallows he had planned for Mordecai.

(I) MARY THE HIGHLY FAVORED AND JOSEPH THE OBEDIENT, AND :(II) ZACHARIAS AND ELIZABETH THE RIGHTEOUS COUPLE

This final episode is a befitting end to this book. Because of the nature of the relationship between Our Lord and Savior Jesus and John the Baptist, this episode couldn't be separated into two. It is a summary demonstration that nothing is impossible with God. He unlocks the womb of an old barren woman, and He empowers a virgin to experience Divine Conception. The episode further shows that God is Love. God could only bring His Son Jesus to earth through this humble manner of a virgin birth in a manger only because the Almighty loves us. He so loved the world that He gave His one and only Son, so that everyone who believes in Him will not perish but have eternal life, John3:16. *THIS IS THE ULTIMATE DEFINITION OF LOVE.*

CONCLUSION

Throughout the Old Testament millennia and the 2000 years following the Great Deliverance by Jesus Christ, the Biblical message of creation remains heart- warming and so spiritually uplifting:

And God said, Let us make man in _our image_, after _our likeness_: ....

 So God created man in his own image, in the image of God created he him; <u>male and female created he them</u>.

 And God blessed them....[50]

 And the LORD God said, It is not good that the man should be alone; I will make him an help meet for him.

 And the rib, which the LORD God had taken from man, made he a woman, and brought her unto the man. And Adam said this is now bone of my bones, and flesh of my flesh: she shall be called Woman, because she was taken out of Man.[51]

---

[50] Genesis 1:26-28 King James Version (KJV)

[51] Genesis 2:18-23 King James Version (KJV)

Therefore, God's scheme of creation and His plans for us would be incomplete without a woman. The woman, therefore, should occupy a place of warmth, love, and respect in man's heart. Certainly, and at the minimum, a woman deserves the opportunity to live the life that Christ died for us to live without any manly impediment. From the scripture above, it is obvious that when we commit violence, rape, and any kind of atrocity against women, we are cannibalizing the "...bone of our bones and flesh of our flesh."

As God is good to us, all the time, we, men, should do that which is good to our mothers and grandmothers, to our sisters, daughters and our wives; furthermore, we, men should ensure that we live a life of righteousness particularly in respect of our women. With this as our starting point, we can easily learn to love ourselves, love each other, and truly love God Almighty and thereby obey Him and be empowered to refrain from all acts of wickedness.

PRAYER FOR POSTERITY

May posterity – irrespective of race, irrespective of color, and irrespective of culture, sophistication or level of economic development – May they put love and respect first for their mothers, their sisters, their wives or girlfriends, their daughters, and all the world's women. May the future of our world be in the hands of a generation who have compassion for gender values according to God's purpose for inclusion rather than exclusion of women; and they can then uncompromisingly pursue, value, and enjoy peace. In Jesus Christ's Name we pray, Amen.

ABOUT THE AUTHOR

L. W. Ralitsoele: Born 20th April, 1942 in Soweto Johannesburg. He received a scholarship from USAID. Did MBA at AU in Washington D.C. He is married. Mission: To serve God in poverty reduction. Experience: High School Teacher, Government Execu tive. Manager: Private Sector Development. Skills: creativity, honesty, Jesus inspiration, positive attitude, confidence. Interests: Bible Study and Walking.